Machine Lear for Beginners: Make Your Own Recommender System

Machine Learning for Beginners Series

Published by Scatterplot Press

Oliver Theobald

TABLE OF CONTENTS

FOREWORD

Recommender systems dictate the stream of content displayed to us each day and their impact on online behavior is second to none. From relevant friend suggestions on Facebook to product recommendations on Amazon, there's no missing their presence and online sway. Whether you agree or disagree with this method of marketing, there's no arguing its effectiveness. If mass adoption doesn't convince you, take a look at what you've recently viewed and bought online. There's a strong chance that at least some of your online activities, including finding this book, originated from algorithm-backed recommendations.

These data-driven systems are eroding the dominance of traditional search while aiding the discoverability of items that might not otherwise have been found. As a breakaway branch of machine learning, it's more important than ever to understand how these models work and how to code your own basic recommender system.

This book is designed for beginners with partial background knowledge of data science and machine learning, including statistics and computing programming using Python. If this is your first foray into data science, you may want to spend a few hours to read my first book *Machine Learning for Absolute Beginners* before you get started here.

DATASETS USED IN THIS BOOK

For issues accessing and downloading these datasets, please contact the author at oliver.theobald@scatterplotpress.com

Goodbooks-10k Datasets (Chapter 6)

These two datasets contain information about books and user ratings collected from www.goodreads.com. The first dataset contains book ratings from individual users, while the second dataset contains information about individual books such as their average rating, number of five-star ratings, ISBN number, author, etc.

https://www.kaggle.com/sriharshavogeti/collaborative-recommender-system-on-goodreads/data

Advertising Dataset (Chapter 7)

This dataset contains fabricated information about the features of users responding to online advertisements, including their gender, age, location, daily time spent online, and whether they clicked on the advertisement. The dataset was created by Udemy course instructor Jose Portilla of Pierian Data and is used in his course *Python for Data Science and Machine Learning Bootcamp*.

https://www.kaggle.com/fayomi/advertising/data

Melbourne Housing Market (Chapter 8)

This third dataset contains data on house, unit, and townhouse prices in Melbourne, Australia. This dataset comprises data scraped from publicly available listings posted weekly on www.domain.com.au. The full dataset contains 14,242 property listings and 21 variables including address, suburb, land size, number of rooms, price, longitude, latitude, postcode, etc.

https://www.kaggle.com/anthonypino/melbourne-housing-market/

INTRODUCING SCIKIT-LEARN

Scikit-learn is the core library for general machine learning. It offers an extensive repository of shallow algorithms[1] including logistic regression, decision trees, linear regression, gradient boosting, etc., a broad range of evaluation metrics such as mean absolute error, as well as data partition methods including split validation and cross validation. Scikit-learn is also used to perform a number of important machine learning tasks including training the model and using the trained model to predict the test data.

The following table is a brief overview of common terms and functions used in machine learning from Scikit-learn.

---

[1] Shallow algorithms can be roughly characterized as non-deep learning approaches that aren't structured as part of a sophisticated network. In shallow learning, the model predicts outcomes directly from the input features, whereas in deep learning, the output is based on the output of preceding layers in the model and not directly from the input features.

Term	Explanation	Code Example
estimator	An estimator refers to a set hyperparameter value, such as C in Support Vector Machines, n neighbors in k-NN or n number of trees in random forests. Set prior to training your model, the estimator maps each hyperparameter value to the learning algorithm.	``` model = ensemble.GradientBoostingRegressor(n_estimators = 150, learning_rate = 0.1, max_depth = 30, min_samples_split = 4, min_samples_leaf = 6, max_features = 0.6, loss = 'huber') ``` Each of the seven hyperparameters represents an individual estimator for the algorithm gradient boosting.
fit()	After setting the estimator(s), the fit() function is used to run the learning algorithm on the training data and train the prediction model.	``` model = KNeighborsClassifier(n_neighbors=5) model.fit(X_train, y_train) ``` This code excerpt fits the k-NN model to the X and y training data.
predict()	After the model has been trained, the predict() function uses the newly trained model to make predictions using the X test data. In the case of supervised learning, this involves using the model to predict the labels or values of the X test data.	``` prediction = model.predict(X_test) ``` In this example, the trained model is asked to predict the X test data and is assigned as a new variable ("prediction").
transform()	The transform() function is used to modify the data before feeding it to a learning algorithm (pre-processing). This means taking the original data and outputting a transformed version of it. Examples include normalization, standardization, dimensionality reduction.	``` from sklearn.preprocessing import StandardScaler scaler = StandardScaler() scaler.fit(X_train) X_train = scaler.transform(X_train) ``` After importing StandardScaler, we can use the transform method to rescale/standardize the X training data. The transformed training data is scaled to unit variance with a mean of zero and can now be fit to a learning algorithm.

Table 1: Overview of key Scikit learn terms and functions

1

INTRODUCTION

It wasn't long ago that surfing the Internet was a standalone task that fell into our daily schedule like reading the newspaper or putting out the trash. For an hour or two, we disconnected the phone line and listened to the screech of the modem link to the world wide web.

Load speed was slow, and there was a drawn-out thought process that preceded each click. Waiting twenty seconds or longer for a page to render placed a heavy time penalty on selecting the wrong link. But as wireless broadband Internet infiltrated more homes, schools, and offices, online behavior changed and our browsing habits started to become more brazen. Oops! Clicked on the wrong link? No problem. Jab the "Back" button and you're right back where you started. A few seconds might be lost but as Steve Krug explains in the book *Don't Make Me Think: A Common Sense Approach to Web Usability*, "there's not much of a penalty for guessing wrong."[2] Krug clarifies that users don't choose the best option but rather the "first reasonable option," a strategy he calls "satisficing."

---

[2] Steve Krug, "Don't Make Me Think, Revisited: A Common Sense Approach to Web Usability," *New Riders*, 3rd Edition, 2014.

"As soon as we find a link that seems like it might lead to what we're looking for, there's a very good chance that we'll click on it," explains Krug.[3]

Design trends would also further help streamline user habits. As Internet users became more familiar with site navigation, web designers caught on that it was better to incorporate existing design norms than attempting to reinvent the wheel. Intuitively, web users knew to hone in on the top-right corner for the "Log In" button, to the website footer for contact details and more menu options, and to whatever button appeared the biggest and brightest as a clue for what to click next.

But with this newfound confidence, we lost some of our behavioral programming from the offline world, such as the ability to browse auxiliary content and digest information. Inpatient and impervious to distraction, our attention spans plummeted and "satisficing" took hold. As Mike McGuire, vice president of the technology research firm Gartner, explains, "If there's not something else there surfacing that meets your interest beyond what you initially dialed in for, then you're out."[4]

Realizing this problem, the Internet companies saw they needed a new way to hook attention and curb our smash-and-grab mentality. They knew it was impossible to design web content

---

[3] Steve Krug, "Don't Make Me Think, Revisited: A Common Sense Approach to Web Usability," *New Riders*, 3rd Edition, 2014.
[4] Timothy Stenovec, "Netflix Launches Profiles, Finally Realizing How People Really Watch Movies On It," *The Huffington Post*, accessed April 2, 2018, https://www.huffingtonpost.com/2013/08/01/netflix-profiles_n_3685876.html/.

catering to every user's individual needs and designing content tailored to a general audience merely made it easy for users to skim past on the way to what they came for. Flashing banners, intrusive pop-up windows, and hierarchical lists of popular or recent articles were tried but nothing could quite compare with a deliberately more mathematical approach. While it took almost two decades to perfect, this new approach would radically change online browsing habits and return the advantage to the platforms that could master this emerging and powerful technique.

The answer was a system of algorithms called a *recommender system*; systems that could predict what an individual user liked and mirror related items to the user in highly visible sections of the website. Author Robert Green explains the psychological power of mirrors in his book *The 48 Laws of Power*.

"You look deep into the souls of other people, fathom their innermost desires, their values, their tastes, their spirit and reflect it back to them. Making yourself into a kind of mirror image. Your ability to reflect their psyche back to them gives you great power over them."[5]

While the theory was sound, it took time for the machine algorithms to work. Rudimentary systems evolved in the early 1990s and were refined in the mid-1990s as the web matured into a medium for online commerce. The early exponents of

---

[5] Robert Green, "The 48 Laws of Power," *Profile Books*, New Edition, 2010.

these systems were Dotcom companies like GroupLens who built models to predict a reader's interest in online news articles.[6]

Amazon was another front-runner to the trend. Understanding the potency of user data to drive operational decisions, the Seattle-based company used machine-generated recommendations as a tool to push relevant products to customers. Their early recommendations were crude and clumsy, relying on tags to serve items based on related categories and keywords. Then, in a series of tactical moves to improve the way they recommended products to users, the company made a deal with AOL in the early 2000s. The deal granted Amazon access to operate the technology behind AOL's e-commerce platform and acquire access to an important source of data. While AOL viewed its users' data in terms of its primary value (recorded sales data), Amazon identified a secondary value that would improve its ability to push personalized product recommendations to users on the Amazon marketplace.

Armed with this new source of data, Amazon's product recommendations became progressively sophisticated as different algorithms and filtering techniques attached to the site like a molecule chain. The use of recommender systems contributed to Amazon's expanding market share and played a

---

[6] The research team at GroupLens also released a number of datasets to the public at a time when real datasets were hard to come by.

critical role in helping niche authors on the platform find new readers.

In 1988 Joe Simpson published a mountain climbing book titled *Touching the Void* that documented his near-death experience scaling the Andes in Peru. According to Chris Anderson, the author of *The Long Tail*, Simpson's book received positive reviews but struggled to maintain attention post its release. A decade later, another mountaineering book, *Into Thin Air* written by Jon Krakauer, was released and enjoyed initial success on the Amazon platform. Recognizing a statistically significant combination of customers who purchased both books, Amazon began promoting *Touching the Void* to customers who bought *Into the Air* and vice versa. This sparked a sales revival of the former that would eventually eclipse the popularity of its more recent contemporary.[7]

This case study is one of many examples exhibiting the power of algorithms to aid discoverability and support content creators who would otherwise fall from view without a big marketing budget.

Owing to their effectiveness, Amazon's recommender algorithms augmented control over the e-commerce platform. This, though, came at a cost because like others in the book retail industry, Amazon relied on human editors to recommend books to

---

[7] Chris Anderson, "The Long Tail," *Wired*, accessed April 30, 2018, https://www.wired.com/2004/10/tail/.

customers. Amazon's editors drew on their expert knowledge of literature sold on the platform and the Amazon customer base to propose recommendations. For a time, it seemed that both the in-house reviewers and the faceless algorithms could work together—not in unison but at least side-by-side. The fate of Amazon's in-house editors was later settled after the company ran tests comparing sales data.

"Eventually the editors were presented with the precise percentage of sales Amazon had to forgo when it featured their reviews online," explain the authors of *Big Data: A Revolution That Will Transform How We Live, Work and Think,* Viktor Mayer-Schönberger and Kenneth Cukier.[8] Today a third of all of Amazon's sales are thought to emanate from its recommendation engine[9] and the original team of in-house book reviewers has long since disbanded. Amazon now dominates the online book business and has forced many traditional giants to the side or expelled them from the publishing industry.

The effectiveness of algorithm-based recommender systems appears to be having a similar effect on online organizations without the same data-driven mindset. In April 2018, the founders of Inbound.org (the "Hacker News" of the content

---

[8] Viktor Mayer-Schonberger & Kenneth Cukier, "Big Data: A Revolution That Will Transform How We Live, Work and Think," *Hodder & Stoughton*, 2013.
[9] Ian Mackenzie, Chris Meyer, and Steve Noble, "How retailers can keep up with consumers," *McKinsey*, accessed April 21, 2018, https://www.mckinsey.com/industries/retail/our-insights/how-retailers-can-keep-up-with-consumers/.

marketing world) sent an email to subscribers explaining their uneasy decision to shut down the site. Inbound.org Co-founder, Dharmesh Shah, sighted social recommendation engines as one of the obstacles to the site's growth.

"...it's time to say farewell to inbound.org, as we know it. Why? Primarily because though the concept of a community is compelling—the core use case of user-curated marketing content is not. My suspicion is that it's because of the way people find and share content has changed a great deal since inbound.org's inception. With the growth of messaging platforms and the sharpening of social recommendation engines, content curation via community submission and voting is useful—but not indispensable."[10]

In 2011, the co-author of Mosaic, co-founder of Netscape, and partner of Silicon Valley VC firm Andreessen Horowitz, Marc Andreessen, declared, "software is eating the world." In 2018, it seems that recommender systems are having a similar impact on the web.

In the next chapter, we'll move past the macro impact of recommender systems and begin to break down their unique features and ability to predict user preferences.

---

[10] Dharmesh Shah, "Farewell to inbound.org and hello to Growth Hub," *Inbound.org*, accessed April 20, 2018, https://inbound.org/blog/farewell-to-inboundorg-and-hello-to-growth-hub-growthorg/.

2

THE ANATOMY

Before we dive into exploring specific algorithms, we first need to examine how recommender systems fit into the broader landscape of data science.

Data science, itself, is an interdisciplinary field of methodologies and algorithms to extract knowledge or insight from data. Within the vast space of data science lies the popular field of artificial intelligence (AI), which is the ability of machines to simulate intellectual tasks. A prominent sub-field of artificial intelligence is machine learning, among other sub-fields such as perception, and search and planning. Recommender systems fall under the banner of machine learning and to some extent data mining.

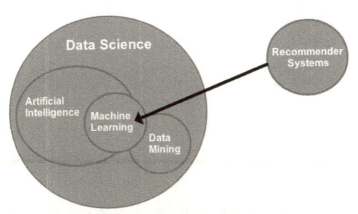

Figure 1: Visual representation of data-related fields and sub-fields

Machine learning applies statistical methods to improve performance based on previous experience. While the programmer is responsible for feature selection and setting the model's hyperparameters (algorithm learning settings), the machine assumes the majority of the work and the important decision-making process. Decisions are formed using advanced pattern recognition, and, typically, through managing far more variables than humans can mentally visualize. This process of combing data for patterns and forming predictions is known as self-learning and represents a major distinction from traditional computer programming where computers are designed to perform set tasks in response to pre-programmed commands. Using machine learning principles, computers don't strictly need to receive an "input command" to perform a task but rather "input data."

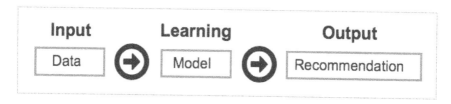

Figure 2: Basic model representation of machine learning

Data mining is the process of discovering and unearthing patterns contained in complex datasets. Popular self-learning algorithms such as *k*-means clustering, decision trees, and regression analysis are applied in both data mining and machine learning. But whereas machine learning focuses on incremental and ongoing problem-solving using models that evolve with experience, data mining concentrates on cleaning up large datasets to create valuable insight at a set point in time.

Data mining is suitable for tasks such as cleaning up historical road traffic data to find the optimal route for a delivery fleet based on past experience. Data mining describes what happened in the past, whereas machine learning uses the past to predict the future and refines its predictions over time based on experience and the process of self-learning.

Recommender systems draw on both machine learning and data mining techniques, but machine learning models are generally more effective because user preferences develop over time. Secondly, data mining is less conducive to tasks with a limited amount of data. In many recommender scenarios, there's sparse upfront data regarding the individual user and their known preferences. Machine learning, though, can be used to make inferences and gradually learn from user behavior and optimize recommendations through extensive trial and error.

Let's now talk about the actual algorithms. First, recommender systems shouldn't be mistaken as a single algorithm or even a family of related algorithms. Unlike decision trees, regression analysis, and clustering analysis (three separate families of algorithms), recommender systems are a mismatch of algorithms united under one common goal: to make relevant recommendations. Whether it's logistic regression, nearest neighbors clustering or principal component analysis, recommender systems rely on the algorithm(s) that best recommends items to users.

Second, recommender systems can be broken down into two overarching methodologies: **collaborative filtering** and **content-based filtering**.

Content-based filtering techniques, also known as item-based filtering, recommend similar items to an individual based on items the user has purchased or consumed in the past. Under this logic, a user who enjoys watching five cat videos is likely to watch a sixth cat video if it is recommended to them.

Collaborative filtering, meanwhile, recommends items to an individual based on the items purchased or consumed by other users with shared interests. For instance, YouTube fans of cat videos may also like to watch fitness videos. In this particular case, the items (cat video and fitness video) have no direct relationship to each other in terms of genre or keywords found in their descriptions and metadata. The YouTube recommender will nevertheless suggest fitness videos to cat enthusiasts based on the behavior of similar users. Amazon and other online platforms often label this approach on their website as "See what other users bought." Reflecting the wisdom of the crowd is another way of thinking about collaborative filtering. However, this isn't to say that collaborative filtering is a blind framework for identifying popular items like a top ten list. More accurately, it's a method to match items who share some form of popular association among similar types of users.

A well-used example highlighting the difference between collaborative and content-based filtering is the side-by-side comparison of Last.fm and Pandora Radio. Both music platforms use recommender systems to feed songs to listeners, but where Last.fm draws on collaborative filtering, Pandora Radio employs a content-based approach.

Last.fm plays songs based on what artists and individual tracks the user has listened to in the past and compares this information with the listening behavior of similar users. If other users with a similar taste in music as the target user go through a phase of regularly listening to Billy Joel tracks, Last.fm is likely to recommend Billy Joel songs to the target user based on the taste of those similar users. By tracking the interests of similar users, Last.fm also serves music that users may not directly find on their own.

Pandora's approach to song selection generates less diverse results because it looks exclusively at the listener's taste in music and generates a playlist based on similar content features. This might mean pairing songs from related genres or music vintages. If you're not familiar with Pandora, then you might have noticed a similar phenomenon occurring on YouTube. If you watch music videos from the early 2000s, the site typically recommends other popular music videos from that era and not Billy Joel's song Piano Man from 1977 or Macklemore's Thrift Shop hit from 2014.

As discussed in later chapters, there is a constant trade-off between applying collaborative filtering and content-based filtering. Using collaborative filtering, for example, requires a significant amount of upfront data about users to produce effective recommendations. This situation is known as the *cold-start problem*, which can also affect content-based filtering where there's insufficient profiling of new items. We'll explore the specific advantages and disadvantages as well as the practical application of these two methodologies in Chapter 6 and Chapter 7 (collaborative filtering) and Chapter 8 (content-based filtering). Beyond these two recommender frameworks, there are many other techniques that complement or serve as adaptations to content-based and collaborative filtering techniques.

The Hybrid Approach

A popular alternative to collaborative and content-based filtering is the hybrid approach, which draws on a combination of techniques to serve useful recommendations. The amalgamation of methods and the flexibility built into this approach helps to soften the drawbacks of using a single methodology.

Hybrid recommender systems also benefit from the ability and flexibility to combine multiple data sources and data types. Ordinal data values such as item ratings, for example, are generally used for collaborative based-filtering, whereas continuous variables such as item price and size are more suitable for content-based filtering. A hybrid solution enables one to pipe both data inputs and then segment analysis through a curated selection of techniques.

In practice, a hybrid recommender system operates by running as a unified model or by separating content-based and collaborative filtering or other methods and then combining the predictions. Many popular online platforms including Netflix rely on this hybrid approach.

Knowledge-based Recommenders

Knowledge-based systems provide item recommendations based on a user's needs and relevant information. This normally works on an inference basis, where the system makes recommendations based on unique knowledge about the user.

Amazon, for example, leverages its knowledge of books a user has recently read on their Kindle device to send emails recommending other titles from the author, such as a sequel or other books by the same author.

Another effective demonstration of knowledge-based recommenders is the constant flow of advertisements that reverberate and pursue you after a Google search. Using the same techniques they use to recommend videos, YouTube can serve advertisements based on specific knowledge gained from other platforms such as your Google search history.

Knowledge-based recommenders closely resemble content-based recommenders, and the demarcation line between the two methods can be difficult to discern.[11] Knowledge-based systems, however, are unique because they enable users to specify what they want directly and aren't reliant on the historical data of interactions between items and users.[12]

Knowledge-based recommenders are also highly effective at recommending rare items. This includes rarely purchased or consumed items related to tourism, real estate, relocation, car rental, legal services, and other less frequent business scenarios. As there's generally limited historical data about a user's preference for such items, it's difficult for content-based filtering to generate useful recommendations or even anticipate the existence of such needs. Knowledge-based systems, though, excel at recommending relevant items without the aid of historical data, such as the once-in-a-lifetime need for a graduation gown.

Knowledge, though, can be a double-edged sword. If the information is sensitive and collected through covert means, such as paid data acquisition from a third-party, that knowledge

---

[11] Charu C. Aggarwal, "Recommender Systems: The Textbook," *Springer International Publishing*, 2016.
[12] Charu C. Aggarwal, "Recommender Systems: The Textbook," *Springer International Publishing*, 2016.

doubles as a breach of user privacy. This can cause problems both from an ethical standpoint and potentially from a legal point of view.

For users that share a laptop or user account, the unintended consequences of knowledge-based systems can be harmful and may cross the line of user privacy. A user's search for "divorce attorney" or "guidance for dealing with depression," may be detected by their otherwise uninformed partner or children through subsequent advertisements and online content recommendations.

Finally, as knowledge-based systems require highly specific information about user needs, they can be difficult for smaller companies to develop and implement.

Demographic Recommenders

Demographic recommenders deliver recommendations based on user stereotypes and are typically combined with other methods such as knowledge-based recommenders to build a hybrid model. Regular returning users, for example, might be served different recommendations to those of infrequent users. Other user profiles might be generated based on spending patterns among a specific demographic group or even by what football team they support.

The key to this technique is data collection and gathering sufficient information about the target user from signup forms or user profile pages. Alternatively, data might be collected through observation such as the location of the user's IP address, online spending, and saved cookies to discern whether they have visited the site before, and if so, how frequently.

While demographic recommenders may appear similar to knowledge-based systems, they rely on different types of data for input. Whereas knowledge-based systems focus on situational information, such as the user's need to buy a car, demographic recommenders are dependent on the characteristics of the user, which are more stable and reliable over time.

Mobile-based Recommenders

Given the ubiquitous nature of Internet-enabled mobile devices and smartphones, mobile recommenders are a rapidly emerging branch of recommender system and serve recommendations based on users' geographic location.

This service is available on Facebook, where advertisers can send targeted ads to users active in a new geographic area. A tourist arriving in Australia, for example, might receive recommendations to visit a local brewery 25 kilometers from their current location. Visits to an out-of-town brewery are often a one-time experience, but for the brewery, targeting newcomers to the local area provides an evergreen market for targeted ad campaigns.

As the technology used to capture real-time insights through mobile devices develops, collaborative filtering is expected to become more integrated into mobile recommender systems. The awkward composition of heterogeneous data, though, remains a bottleneck to expanding the use of these systems. As the data collected from mobiles is retrieved from a range of different devices, extra processing such as spatial and temporal autocorrelation is required. In addition, mobile recommender systems need to factor in a considerable amount of context-based information to produce useful recommendations. This includes consideration of local traffic, weather conditions, item availability, and so forth. There's little use in recommending a tourist to visit a local brewery if public transport is not available. The logical solution to this issue is to combine a knowledge-based recommender system with a mobile recommender and utilize information about the user's browsing activity (e.g., local car hire website) to inform its recommendations for local activities.

Other variants of recommender systems not explored in this chapter include:

- **constraint-limited recommenders** (e.g., bound to a user's specified budget or vacation dates),

- **time-sensitive recommenders** (e.g., the time of year or time of day). Pop-tarts at Walmart in the U.S., for example, sell well with essential storm supplies in the lead-up to a storm. Pop-tarts, however, are not necessarily a popular purchase choice with storm supplies at other times of the year.

- **location-based recommenders** (arguably the same as mobile-based recommenders),
- **group-based recommenders** that aggregate individual preferences to recommend content or activities to a group of users (e.g., music played at a bar, advertisements played on giant screens in shopping departments or restaurant recommendations for families), and
- **social recommenders** based on social structures and mutual relationships (e.g., key opinion leader identification on Twitter or friend suggestions on social media based on mutual friends).

Other recommender system approaches set to become more prominent in the future are explored in Chapter 11.

3

SETTING UP A SANDBOX

ENVIRONMENT

Now that you're familiar with the theoretical framework of recommender systems, it's time to turn attention to building a prediction model. For the exercises presented in this book, we'll be using the programming language Python, which is quick to learn and popular among data scientists.

If you don't have programming expertise or any experience coding in Python, don't worry. The key purpose of these exercises is to understand the methodology and steps behind building a basic recommender system. As for our development environment, we'll be installing Jupyter Notebook, which is an open-source web application that allows for the editing and sharing of code notebooks.

The remainder of this chapter is dedicated to installing Jupyter Notebook. If you've used Jupyter Notebook in the past or have read my earlier title *Machine Learning for Absolute Beginners*, you may wish to skip this section and proceed to the next chapter.

Downloading Jupyter Notebook

Jupyter Notebook can be installed using the Anaconda Distribution or Python's package manager, pip. As an experienced Python user, you may wish to install Jupyter Notebook via pip, and there are instructions available on the Jupyter Notebook website (http://jupyter.org/install.html) outlining this option. For beginners, I recommend choosing the Anaconda Distribution option, which offers an easy click-and-drag setup (https://www.anaconda.com/products/individual/).

This installation option will direct you to the Anaconda website. From there, you can select your preferred installation for Windows, macOS, or Linux. Again, you can find instructions available on the Anaconda website based on your chosen operating system.

After installing Anaconda on your machine, you'll have access to a number of data science applications including rstudio, Jupyter Notebook, and graphviz for data visualization through the Anaconda application. To proceed, you need to select Jupyter Notebook by clicking on "Launch" inside the Jupyter Notebook tab.

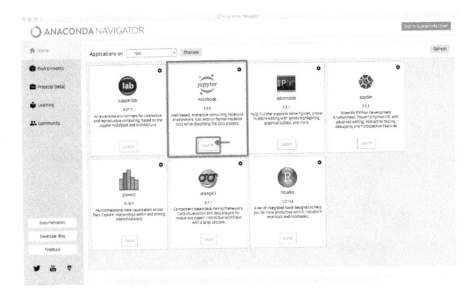

Figure 3: The Anaconda Navigator portal

To initiate Jupyter Notebook, run the following command from the Terminal (for Mac/Linux) or Command Prompt (for Windows):

```
jupyter notebook
```

Terminal/Command Prompt then generates a URL for you to copy and paste it into your web browser.

Figure 4: Copy URL and paste it into the browser

Copy and paste the generated URL into your browser to access Jupyter Notebook. Once you have Jupyter Notebook open in your browser, click on "New" in the top right-hand corner of the web application to create a new notebook project, and then select "Python 3."

Figure 5: Inside Jupyter Notebook

You've now successfully set up a sandbox environment with your web browser using Jupyter Notebook. This means that the following experimentation and code changes won't affect the resources outside of this isolated testing environment.

Figure 6: A new Jupyter notebook ready for coding

4

WORKING WITH DATA

Data for a typical recommender system consists of two entities in the form of "users" and "items" organized in what's called a *utility matrix*. While it sounds intimidating, a utility matrix is a simple pivot table containing pairs of values, such as an individual user and their ratings for given items.

	Movie 1	Movie 2	Movie 3	Movie 4	Movie 5	Movie 6	Movie 7
User 1					1		1
User 2		4		5		5	
User 3		3	2	5			
User 4				2	3	4	
User 5		3					
User 6				4			5
User 7			5	5	5		

Table 2: Example of a utility matrix

Users are often arranged vertically in rows, and items are placed horizontally in columns. The preferences of each user to a given item can be found by searching for the relevant column. The aligning cell depicts the user's preference for that item, which is generally represented as a numeric value. In the case of the evaluation systems used by Netflix and Amazon, these values are expressed as categorical integers (whole numbers) between one and five that specify user tastes.

However, not all user preference systems boil down to a simple score between one and five. On Facebook, for example, users can only "like" posts that appear in their social feed. As a binary feature, these actions can be converted into numeric values using a technique called one-hot encoding, which transforms variables into binary form, represented as "1" or "0"—"True" or "False." In the case of Facebook, "Likes" can be encoded as "1" and the absence of a "like" or "unknown" (where the value is null) is encoded as "0."

Before One-hot Encoding

Customer	Customer Action Status
Customer 1	Purchased
Customer 2	Added to Shopping Cart
Customer 3	No Action Taken

After One-hot Encoding

Customer	Purchased	Shopping_Cart	No_Action
Customer 1	1	0	0
Customer 2	0	1	0
Customer 3	0	0	1

Table 3: Example of one-hot encoding

In situations where users don't offer feedback in the form of a rating, like, or other action to express their preference—the value is referred to as "sparse," meaning the value is unknown. This is a common occurrence on the web, as most people don't review every item they consume. Like most users, you probably only submit a rating and share direct feedback for a fraction of the items you consume and purchase online. Given the heavy presence of null values in a utility matrix, it can sometimes be difficult to generate accurate predictions.

There are two general methodologies to counter the problem of a sparse matrix. The first method is to accelerate the collection of user feedback by enticing users to leave a review, a "like," or other forms of feedback that help to define user tastes. This method, though, is generally met with hard resistance or false information provided by the user in exchange for a reward.

The second approach is to generate inferences about user preferences through indirect feedback, known as *latent variables*. These are variables that are not directly observed but are inferred through observing other known variables. The most obvious indication of a user's preferences is to analyze their historical purchase data, which has become more available with the growth of online commerce and smartphone usage.

Other indirect ways of discerning users' preferences are whether they watched a video clip through to its completion, shared an online article with friends, and time-on-page (the time spent by the user on a single web page). Importantly, these examples don't require direct feedback or additional effort by the user and are therefore easier to collect in high volume.

Text mining and sentiment analysis can also be utilized to review user preferences contained inside text-based comments pertaining to video, news, and other digital content but these collection techniques are more advanced and resource-intensive to run.

When collecting data, it's important to keep in mind that utility matrixes work optimally with values that clearly categorize a user's preference, including ordinal variables such as the 1-5 star rating system or binary/Boolean variables such as Facebook "Likes." Ordinal variables are values categorized in a clear sequence, whereas Boolean variables are binary values that produce one of two set outcomes, such as yes/no, true/false, 0/1. To categorize user preferences, data scientists sometimes need to create a Boolean or ordinal threshold for other variable types. For instance, if a user watches a video clip through (or near to) its completion, this action can be labeled as "1" (the user liked the video). If the user abandons the video halfway through or below a set playback threshold (of say 80%), then it can be labeled as "0" (the user didn't like the video or their preference is unknown).

This technique, though, generally fails to compare with the convenience and precision of systems that directly collect data from the user as ordinal or Boolean variables. This is because the transformation of other variable types can come with interpretation bias. Unlike ordinal and binary variables, it's challenging to define user preferences based on continuous variables (infinite/not limited to a set range of values) such as time spent on the page. As an example, how do we know if a user liked an 800-word blog post that took seven minutes to read compared to another blog of similar length which took five and a half minutes to read? Perhaps the first blog was poorly written, and it took the user longer to digest. Alternatively, maybe the user found the information they needed from the second blog and then quickly jumped to another website to complete their tax return or submit a visa application. Ordinal variables, on the other hand, clearly communicate user preferences based on predefined values that express whether a user liked a given item. It's no coincidence that Amazon and Netflix—two of the most prolific exponents of recommendation systems—built a library of explicit user preferences organized into a five-star evaluation system.

Keeping your utility matrix as objective and simple as possible, including the use of ordinal or binary values generated directly by the user, also makes your data more accurate and straightforward to process. Online platforms developing recommender systems can therefore learn from Amazon and Netflix's success when designing their own user interface. Also, it's essential that data scientists have partial input concerning the design of the website or app being developed based on the data types they wish to analyze in the future.

5

DATA REDUCTION

Recommender systems rely on data as input, and this can be collected through an assortment of channels including sign-up forms, web crawling, logs of online user behavior, IP and geographic tracking, and many other channels.

There are two major categories of input data: **structured data** and **unstructured data**. Structured data is information that resides in a fixed field within a record or file. This generally comprises information stored in rows and columns with a defined schema (a blueprint of how the database is constructed). Examples of structured data include event registration information stored in the rows and columns of a spreadsheet or user profiles stored in a relational database, including users' personal information and shipping address.

Unstructured data or non-structured data is information that doesn't fit neatly into a pre-defined data model or isn't organized in a pre-defined manner. This includes information found in emails, social media posts, word-processing documents, voice recordings, etc. In this book, we focus on structured data stored in rows and columns as exemplified by the utility matrix discussed in the previous chapter.

While structured data is far closer to "production-ready" than unstructured data, it still requires some manipulation and preparation before its ready to analyze. This might entail deleting irrelevant data, redesigning non-numeric values as numeric values, discarding infrequent users/buyers, discarding extremely unpopular items, and reducing the overall quantity of data through column or row compression. If you aren't familiar with the data reduction techniques mentioned so far, don't worry, as we'll cover most of these methods here in this chapter.

First, though, what *is* the purpose of data reduction? In sum, data reduction helps to separate the signal from the noise, reduce total processing time, and minimize the consumption of computational resources. Popular e-commerce platforms and social media networks have up to millions of individual users and items. iTunes and Spotify, alone, have approximately 40+ and 30+ million songs on their platforms respectively.[13] As these sites are working with massive datasets, the computational costs of managing data are significant as well as time-consuming to process. Using data reduction techniques, they can improve the performance, efficiency, and accuracy of their recommender

---

[13] Parker Hall & Brendan Hesse, "Apple Music vs. Spotify: Which is the Streaming King?", *Digital Trends,* accessed April 28, 2018, https://www.digitaltrends.com/music/apple-music-vs-spotify/.

systems by focusing on the data that is most useful to their goals of analysis.

Another reason why data reduction is useful is that it might not be possible to visualize data until after it has been compressed. Having an excessive number of data points or dimensions, greater than three (3-D) or four (4-D) dimensions, can make it difficult or impossible to visualize patterns and regularities in the dataset. The downside of data reduction, though, is a potential dip in accuracy and loss of relevant data, and this trade-off presents a constant challenge for data scientists.

Let's now take a look at specific examples of data reduction.

Row Compression

Row compression involves reducing the volume of rows while attempting to preserve information from the original structure. Rather than outright deleting rows, this might take the form of compressing a large number of rows into a lower number of clusters (groups of data points) based on similar values using a technique called *k*-means clustering. YouTube, for example, has 1.3 billion users. This is not a dataset you want to fiddle with inside an Excel spreadsheet,[14] but using data reduction methods you can reduce the volume of rows into a smaller and more manageable number.

---

[14] By default, an Excel Worksheet can support up to 1,048,576 rows and 16,384 columns of data.

Dimension Reduction

Known also as *descending dimension algorithms*, dimension reduction transforms data from high-dimensional to low-dimensional. This works through the strategic selection of dataset columns. Be wary that this is not a case of deleting columns or the data those columns contain but mathematically transforming data in a way that the information collected is captured using fewer dimensions.

Dimensions are the number of variables characterizing the data, such as the city of residence, country of residence, age, and gender of a user. Up to four variables can be plotted on a scatterplot, but three-dimensional and two-dimensional plots are the easiest for human eyes to interpret.

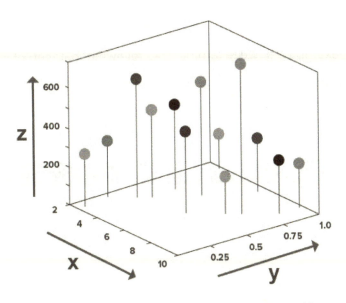

Figure 7: Three-dimensional scatterplot with three variables

The ability to visualize relationships and patterns is convenient for communication purposes but isn't necessary for producing predictions. Models that contain the input of 20 variables cannot be visualized on a scatterplot but can still be used to identify patterns and aid decision-making through binary outputs such as 1 (true) and 0 (false) or numeric predictions.

Beyond the ability to visualize results in four or fewer dimensions, the other benefits of dimension reduction are the reduced consumption of computational resources through processing fewer variables and removing or minimizing the impact of variables that don't have a significant impact on data patterns.

There are several methods for reducing dimensionality, ranging from simple manual manipulation to more sophisticated algorithmic transformations. At the primitive end of the data reduction spectrum, there is the manual approach of merging variables. For example, if we examine the following dataset of user movie ratings, we can use categorization to reduce the total number of variables without deleting existing information.

	The Big Short	Finding Nemo	The Blind Side	Black Panther	Wonder Woman	Moneyball	Coco	Guardians of the Galaxy
User 1	4		4	3		4		5
User 2							4	1
User 3	3		1		5			
User 4					4	4		

Table 4: Original dataset

These eight movies can be reclassified into the following categories:

Michael Lewis Adaptation: The Big Short, The Blind Side, Moneyball

Family: Finding Nemo, Coco

Superhero-Action: Black Panther, Wonder Woman, Guardians of the Galaxy

User ratings for individual movies are then summed and averaged to populate category rating values.

	Michael Lewis Adaptation	Family	Superhero-Action
User 1	4		4
User 2		4	1
User 3	2		5
User 4	4		4

Table 5: Recreated dataset

This transformation captures the information using fewer variables and reduces the number of variables from eight to three. The downside of this transformation is there's now less information regarding specific relationships between individual movies. Thus, rather than recommending movies to users based on other movies, recommendations are formed according to movie categories.

This method is admittedly crude and overtly manual for the purpose of developing sophisticated recommender systems. This is why descending dimension algorithms are a more effective methodology for implementing dimension reduction, as we'll uncover next.

Principal Component Analysis

One of the most popular descending dimension algorithm techniques is principal component analysis (PCA). Known also as *general factor analysis*, PCA examines interrelations among a set of variables and removes components that have the least impact on data variability. This helps to reveal hidden and simplified structures in the data and is often used as a pre-processing step before applying another algorithm.

As with other descending dimension algorithms, PCA is useful for reducing data complexity and visualizing multidimensional data using fewer variables by synthesizing variables into components. The algorithm allows one to take a dataset with a high number of variables, such as 20-30 variables, and find the principal components that have the most impact on data variability. Components are identified through the statistical application of an orthogonal line perpendicular (at a right angle) to the regression hyperplane. The orthogonal line then takes the role of the new y-axis.

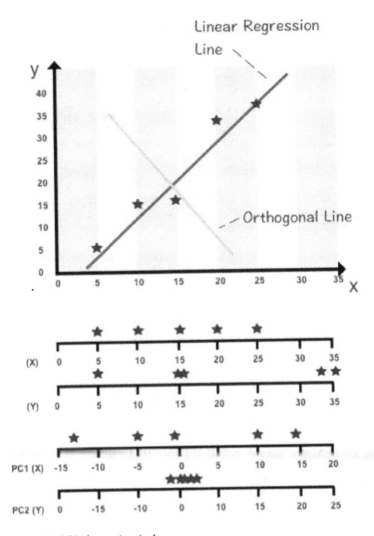

Figure 8: PCA deconstructed

In Figure 8 are four horizontal axes. The first two axes relate the x and y values denoted in the original data plot. The third and fourth axes measure the distance from the new x and y values with the orthogonal line taking the place of the original y-axis.

47

The new x-axis is Principal Component 1 (PC 1), and the new y-axis is Principal Component 2 (PC 2).

Under the new PC1 and PC2 axes (the third and fourth axis), we can see a change in variance amongst the data points. The variance in PC1 has expanded in comparison to the original x values (seen in the first axis). Meanwhile, the variance in PC2 has shrunk significantly as all data points are virtually stacked on top of each other, close to zero.

As PC2 contributes the least to overall variance, we can focus our attention on studying the variance along PC1. While PC1 doesn't contain 100% of the original information, it captures the data points that have the most impact on data patterns and improves computational performance.

In this example, we divided the dataset into two principal components before selecting one principal component. In other scenarios, you might select two or three principal components that contain 75% of the information from a total of ten components. (Of course, insisting on 100% of the information would defeat the purpose of data reduction and maximizing performance.)

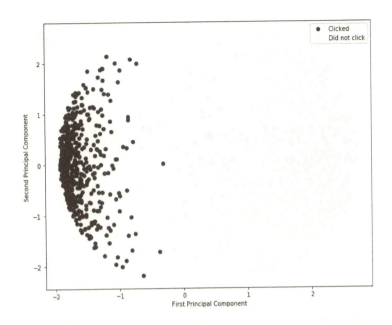

Figure 9: Example of PCA after the isolation of 2 principal components from 7 original features

Like compressing an image to a smaller file format such as JPEG, dimension reduction techniques including PCA do cause some information loss. Thus, although dimension reduction helps to summarize the variability of high-dimensional data and speed up training, it may result in a slight sacrifice to accuracy.

In the next exercise we will use another descending dimension algorithm called singular-value decomposition to compress data to represent generalized user tastes.

6

COLLABORATIVE FILTERING

PART 1

As you'll recall from Chapter 2, recommender systems are not a specific algorithm but rather an application of machine learning and data mining. The two primary architectures for recommending items are **content-based filtering** and **collaborative filtering**. This chapter examines collaborative filtering.

Collaborative filtering recommends items to a user based on analysis of similar users and their preferences, past purchases, ratings or other general behavior. Collaborative filtering can also be split into two methods.

The first method is user-based collaborative filtering, which generates recommendations to a target user based on the historical preferences of similar users. Another way of expressing this is *people similar to you who buy x also buy y.*

In practice, like-minded users are first identified, and their ratings or preferences are then collected and grouped to produce a weighted average. The group's general preferences are used to recommend items to individual users based on the ratings and preferences of their peers. For instance, if a user has never seen a given film or TV series that their peers watched and rated positively, the system will recommend this content item to the user based on peer observation.

The second method is item-based collaborative filtering, which rather than finding users with similar preferences, finds a set of items similar to the target item based on user preferences. For example, Star Wars movies rated highly by a similar audience of users will be matched together as a set and then recommended to other users who like and rate one of the movies in the set. Item-based filtering can therefore be thought of as *people who buy x also buy y.*

The main distinction between the two methods lies in the selection of input. Item-based filtering first takes a given item, finds users who liked that item, and then retrieves other items that those users liked. Conversely, user-based filtering first takes a selected user, finds users similar to that user based on similar ratings, and then recommends items that similar users also liked.

In reality, item-based and user-based collaborative filtering tend to produce similar item recommendations, but user-based filtering can be more accurate for datasets that have a large number of users with esoteric interests. Datasets that have less information regarding user characteristics and tastes, though, are generally more compatible with item-based collaborative filtering.

Let's now review the advantages and drawbacks of collaborative filtering.

Advantages

1) Low knowledge of item characteristics

A major advantage of collaborative filtering is that it doesn't rely on a sophisticated understanding of items and their specific attributes. This saves upfront effort as you don't need to spend time meticulously documenting items. This is especially convenient for online video and audio content items that are generated daily and time-consuming to review and classify.

2) Flexible over the long-term

As collaborative filtering responds directly to user behavior and trends, this technique is generally more flexible than content-based filtering at reacting to changes in user/consumer behavior. Sudden short-term changes in fashion, pop culture, and other trends, though, can be difficult to respond to—at least initially—depending on when the data is collected.

3) Discoverability

Collaborative filtering enables the discoverability of items outside the user's standard periphery as it synthesizes preferences from users they've never met but who share similar interests.

Disadvantages

1) Large-scale user data

A challenge and potential drawback of collaborative filtering is the significant amount of upfront information that is needed to document user preferences. Without this information, collaborative filtering is mostly ineffective, and this can be a challenge for new entrants without an established user base. Obtaining or acquiring data from a comparable platform, as Amazon did via its partnership with AOL, is one strategy to overcome the cold-start problem.

Lastly, the scalability of collaborative systems can be computationally challenging for platforms with a massive number of users.

2) Malicious activity

Collaborative filtering is, unfortunately, highly vulnerable to people gaming the system and doing the wrong thing. This includes driving fake traffic to target items, attacking competitor's items with negative reviews, fabricating online user personas or creating a general system of user actions to cheat the system, also known as a *shilling attack*.

One approach to minimize malicious activity is to limit the model's analysis to user purchases, rather than browsing habits, as the former is more difficult to fabricate. That said, fraudulent online transactions are still common, and unscrupulous actors are continually developing their tactics to game recommender systems.

Mitigating the influence of shilling attacks is an exciting and lucrative area of machine learning to consider as a future career path.

3) Negative reputation

As collaborative filtering relies heavily on extracting users' personal information to execute recommendations to others, the use of such techniques can evoke concerns regarding data privacy (discussed in Chapter 10) and social manipulation. Criticism has surfaced in recent times regarding the 2016 U.S. election and the alleged role Facebook had in sharing user data to a third-party organization as well as their content display algorithms that potentially reinforce political biases and disseminate news stories.

Exercise: Recommending books

In the following exercise we will create an item-based collaborative filtering technique to recommend books based on reader ratings using singular-value decomposition (SVD) and correlation coefficients. A user-based collaborative filtering model will be the focus of the exercise in the next chapter.

Step 1

Let's begin by importing the required libraries for this exercise, which are NumPy, Pandas, and the TruncatedSVD algorithm from

Scikit-learn. (Truncated SVD is generally faster for working with rectangular matrices than standard SVD.)

```
import numpy as np
import pandas as pd
from sklearn.decomposition import TruncatedSVD
```

Step 2

Next, let's import the data. For this exercise, we are using two separate CSV files from the Goodbooks-10k dataset, which contain information regarding books and user ratings collected from www.goodreads.com. The first dataset contains book ratings from individual users, while the second dataset includes information concerning individual books such as the average rating, number of five-star ratings, ISBN, author, etc.

Both datasets are available for download at https://www.kaggle.com/sriharshavogeti/collaborative-recommender-system-on-goodreads/data

```
#Import first dataset and define columns
ratings = pd.read_csv('~/Downloads/ratings.csv')
columns = ['book_id', 'user_id', 'rating']


#Import second dataset and define columns
books = pd.read_csv('~/Downloads/books.csv')
```

```
columns = ['id','book_id', 'best_book_id', 'work_id',

'books_count', 'isbn', 'isbn13', 'authors',

'original_publication_year', 'original_title', 'title',

'language_code', 'average_rating', 'ratings_count',

'work_ratings_count', 'work_text_reviews_count', 'ratings_1',

'ratings_2', 'ratings_3', 'ratings_4', 'ratings_5',

'image_url', 'small_image_url']
```

We next need to combine the two datasets using the `pd.merge` command using Pandas.

```
combined_books_data = pd.merge(ratings, books, on='book_id')
```

From this line of code, we can see that we have merged the two datasets ("ratings" and "books") based on the shared variable "book_id," which is present in both datasets.

Let's now preview the dataset using the `head` command.

```
combined_books_data.head()
```

```
13  combined_books_data = pd.merge(ratings, books, on='book_id')
14
15  combined_books_data.head()
16
```

	book_id	user_id	rating	id	best_book_id	work_id	books_count	isbn	isbn13	authors	...	ratings_count
0	1	314	5	27	1	41335427	275	439785960	9.780440e+12	J.K. Rowling, Mary GrandPré	...	1678823
1	1	439	3	27	1	41335427	275	439785960	9.780440e+12	J.K. Rowling, Mary GrandPré	...	1678823
2	1	588	5	27	1	41335427	275	439785960	9.780440e+12	J.K. Rowling, Mary GrandPré	...	1678823
3	1	1169	4	27	1	41335427	275	439785960	9.780440e+12	J.K. Rowling, Mary GrandPré	...	1678823
4	1	1185	4	27	1	41335427	275	439785960	9.780440e+12	J.K. Rowling, Mary GrandPré	...	1678823

5 rows × 25 columns

Please note that not all columns are visible in this screenshot. The full 25 columns can be viewed by scrolling to the right inside Jupyter Notebook.

Step 3

The third step is to create a utility matrix, which is a pivot table that we'll use to store book ratings made by individual readers.

```
rating_utility_matrix =
combined_books_data.pivot_table(values = 'rating', index =
'user_id', columns = 'title', fill_value = 0)
```

The utility matrix of user ratings (`rating_utility_matrix`) is generated by selecting variables from the `combined_books_data` dataset that we created in the previous step. Individual book titles are expressed horizontally as columns, and individual readers are sequenced vertically as rows. The reader's rating for each book is then placed inside the corresponding cell. Finally, all books that have not been rated are allocated a value of zero using `fill_value = 0`.

We can preview the utility matrix again using the `head` command.

```
rating_utility_matrix.head()
```

```
rating_utility_matrix = combined_books_data.pivot_table(values='rating', index='user_id', columns='title', fill_value=0
rating_utility_matrix.head()
```

title	'Salem's Lot	'Tis (Frank McCourt, #2)	1421: The Year China Discovered America	1776	1984	A Bend in the River	A Bend in the Road	A Brief History of Time	A Briefer History of Time	A Case of Need	...	Women in Love (Brangwen Family, #2)	World War Z: An Oral History of the Zombie War	World Without End (The Kingsbridge Series, #2)	Wuthering Heights	Xenocide (Ender's Saga, #3)	Year of Wonder
user_id																	
2	0	0	0	0	0	0	0	0	0	0	...	0	0	0	0	0	
3	0	0	0	0	0	0	0	0	0	0	...	0	0	0	0	0	
4	0	0	0	0	0	0	0	0	0	0	...	0	0	0	0	0	
7	0	0	0	0	0	0	0	0	0	0	...	0	0	0	0	0	
9	0	0	0	0	0	0	0	0	0	0	...	0	0	0	0	0	

5 rows × 812 columns

This is a classic case of a scarce dataset, as users haven't submitted a rating for each individual item. To overcome this problem, we can compress individual user preferences into a lower number of general user tastes.

Step 4

To compress the values of individual readers, we'll use a descending dimension algorithm called singular-value decomposition (SVD) to convert the total number of individual readers into a limited number of components. Similar to principal component analysis, singular-value decomposition is used to rank the importance of features (dimensions) and reduce a high-dimensional dataset into fewer dimensions while retaining maximum variance.

SVD is used here over PCA as it is more effective at handling missing values treated as zero in a sparse dataset. You can learn more about the mathematical differences between these two descending dimension algorithms from this tutorial by Jonathon Schlens at Google Research (https://arxiv.org/pdf/1404.1100.pdf).

As the primary objective of the recommender system is to suggest relevant books to users, the compression made by SVD does not remove individual readers from the dataset. Instead, reader preferences are compressed into a lower number of components according to similarities between readers to provide general user tastes.

Let's first use the `shape` command to find the total number of rows (users) and columns (books).

```
rating_utility_matrix.shape
```

```
(28906, 812)
```

We can see there are 28,906 individual users and 812 book titles in this dataset. To find a generalized view of users' tastes and preferences, we now want to apply truncated SVD to compress all user ratings into 30 latent variables (per the definition in Chapter 4, *latent variables* are not directly observed but are inferred through observing other known variables).

The first step is to transpose the utility matrix to arrange books in rows and users by columns, as shown below.

```
X = rating_utility_matrix.T
```

Next, use `TruncatedSVD` to compress the number of users in 30 components and fit the algorithm to the transposed utility matrix.

```
SVD = TruncatedSVD(n_components=30)
transposed_matrix = SVD.fit_transform(X)
transposed_matrix.shape
```

```
X = rating_utility_matrix.T

SVD = TruncatedSVD(n_components=30)
transposed_matrix = SVD.fit_transform(X)
transposed_matrix.shape
```

```
(812, 30)
```

Using the `shape` command we can see that the utility matrix has been transposed, so that book titles (812) are now expressed as rows, rather than as columns. The 28,906 readers have been compressed into 30 components and are now expressed as columns.

Step 5

The fifth step is to use a built-in NumPy function to find the correlation in user preferences between a given book and other books based on reader preferences that are now compressed as components. To perform this step, we first need to select a book that we know our target reader likes based on a previous purchase and rating. Thus, let's imagine that the target reader likes the book *1984* written by George Orwell, and he or she leaves a positive 5-star review.

We now want to find other books that are correlated to 1984 based on other user ratings. To do this, we need to use correlation coefficients to identify similar book preferences using a NumPy (np) correlation matrix, which is a table showing correlation coefficients between variables.

```
corr_matrix = np.corrcoef(transposed_matrix)
```

```
books = rating_utility_matrix.columns
books_list = list(books)
```

```
book_1984 = books_list.index('1984')

book_1984
```

```
X = rating_utility_matrix.T

SVD = TruncatedSVD(n_components=30)
transposed_matrix = SVD.fit_transform(X)
transposed_matrix.shape

corr_matrix = np.corrcoef(transposed_matrix)

books = rating_utility_matrix.columns
books_list = list(books)

book_1984 = books_list.index('1984')
book_1984
```

4

This prints the book_id "4", which is the row index position of the book *1984*. Let's now feed this index location into our correlation matrix.

```
corr_1984 = corr_matrix[4]
```

Step 6

The final step is to print a list of book names that have a correlation score of between 0.8 and 1.0. The higher the correlation coefficient, the stronger the relationship a book has to the target book (1984).

```
list(books[(corr_1984 < 1.0) & (corr_1984 > 0.8)])
```

```
corr_1984 = corr_matrix[4]

list(books[(corr_1984 < 1.0) & (corr_1984 > 0.8)])
```
```
['Ivanhoe',
 'Night Over Water',
 'The Great Book of Amber (The Chronicles of Amber, #1-10)',
 'The King of Torts',
 'The Stories of Eva Luna']
```

This returns the books Ivanhoe, Night Over Water, The Great Book of Amber (The Chronicles of Amber, #1-10), The King of Torts, and The Stories of Eva Luna. These five books we can recommend to readers based on the results of our collaborative filtering system. To find more similar books to recommend, we can change the `corr_1984` value to a lower value such as `> 0.7`.

```
corr_1984 = corr_matrix[4]

list(books[(corr_1984 < 1.0) & (corr_1984 > 0.7)])
```

```
['A Christmas Carol',
 'Cry, the Beloved Country',
 "Giada's Family Dinners",
 'Ivanhoe',
 'Naked',
 'Night Over Water',
 'Of Mice and Men',
 'Persuasion',
 'Reading Lolita in Tehran',
 'The Great Book of Amber (The Chronicles of Amber, #1-10)',
 'The King of Torts',
 'The Oresteia  (Ορέστεια, #1-3)',
 'The Stories of Eva Luna',
 'The Terror',
 'The Virgin Blue',
 'Travels with Charley: In Search of America',
 'Wolves of the Calla (The Dark Tower, #5)']
```

COLLABORATIVE FILTERING

PART 2

A large part of recommender systems is deciphering whether a user will be receptive to a recommended item. Singular-value decomposition, as explored in the previous chapter, is a method that can be used to predict user preferences in the case of a sparse dataset. For situations where data is not sparse, we can use other algorithms including logistic regression and Naive Bayes.

The Naive Bayes Classifier—a classification method based on Bayes' theorem—is often used in data science for predicting discrete classes such as spam filtering, A/B testing, sentiment analysis, text classification, and recommender systems.

Bayes' Theorem

Devised in the middle of the 18th Century, Bayes' theorem is used for making inferences based on existing information (conditional probability) and is a central pillar of classical statistics. The formula for Bayes' theorem is shown here:

$$P(A|B) = \frac{P(A)\,P(B|A)}{P(B)}$$

In this formula, **A** and **B** represent two events, and **P** represents the probability of that event occurring. Therefore:

P(A|B) is the probability of **A** given that **B** happens (conditional probability)

P(A) is the probability of **A** (marginal probability)

P(B|A) is the probability of **B** given that **A** happens (conditional probability)

P(B) is the probability of **B** (marginal probability)

Example: Evaluating a home pregnancy test

Let's say that following a clinical test, a drug company advertises a home pregnancy test as 99% accurate in detecting pregnancy among pregnant women. However, of the women who participated in the clinical test only 5.0% were pregnant. This scenario can be expressed as follows:

Event A = Pregnant

Event B = Positive test result

P(A) is the probability of pregnancy without any regard to the result of the test = **5%**

P(B|A) is the probability of a positive test result given the woman is pregnant = **99%**

P(A|B) is the probability of pregnancy given a positive test result = **Unknown**

P(B) is the probability of a positive test result without any regard to whether the woman is pregnant = **Unknown**

$$P(A|B) = \frac{0.05 \times 0.99}{P(B)}$$

We now need to solve for P(A|B) and P(B), which is the probability of pregnancy given a positive test result, and the probability of a positive test result among all participants.

There are two elements to consider for P(B):

1) True-positives: a woman that tests positive (99%) who is pregnant (5%), and

2) False-positives: a woman that tests positive (1%) who isn't pregnant (95%)

P(B) = (0.99 * 0.05 + 0.01 * 0.95)

Let's now add P(B) to the equation to solve for P(A|B):

$$P(A|B) = \frac{(0.05)(0.99)}{0.99 * 0.05 + 0.01 * 0.95}$$

(0.05 * 0.99) / (0.99 * 0.05 + 0.01 * 0.95)

0.0495 / (0.0495 + 0.0095)

0.0495 / 0.059

= 0.8389

Using Bayes' theorem, we've found that the probability of pregnancy given a positive test result P(A|B) is 83.89%, which is significantly lower than the accuracy rate (99%) when only considering pregnant women P(B|A).

This outcome crystalizes when we consider the number of false-positives in respect to the number of true-positives. If we test 1,000 women, we can expect 950 not to be pregnant (95%) and 50 who are pregnant (5%). Among the 950 women who aren't pregnant, we can anticipate 9.5 false positives (950 x 0.01). Simultaneously, among the 50 women who are not pregnant, 49.5 women are expected to test positive (50 x 0.99). Thus, of the 59 (9.5 + 49.5) women who test positive, 49.5/59 or 83.89% women are actually pregnant.

Naive Bayes Classifier

The Naive Bayes algorithm is used as a classifier in machine learning for finding the probability of a class based on conditional probability. This means the algorithm finds the probability of a target class (i.e. "pregnant" or "not pregnant") given the relationship of each input feature (i.e. age, weight, etc) to that class. By multiplying together the conditional probabilities for each feature belonging to a given class across the dataset, the algorithm finds the probability of a single data point belonging to the target class based on its input feature values.

For example, the likelihood of pregnancy given a positive test might be 84% but the probability of a pregnant woman aged over 50 in the dataset is 1%. By multiplying the conditional probabilities for each feature (0.84 x 0.01 = 0.000084), the probability of pregnancy is revised downward, and the woman is likely to be assigned the class of "not pregnant."

Naive Bayes also assumes that the influence of each feature on a given class is independent of other features (and not interdependent). This drastically simplifies the calculations/processing, which is also why the algorithm is called "naive".

We'll now use the Naive Bayes Classifier for user-based collaborative filtering to create a recommender system for online advertisements, where an advertisement is served to a user based on the response rate of other users with similar attributes, including daily time spent on site, age, area income, and daily Internet usage.

Exercise: Matching advertisements to users

Step 1

Step one is to install the required libraries which includes Pandas and GaussianNB from Scikit-learn.

```
import pandas as pd
from sklearn.naive_bayes import GaussianNB
```

Step 2

The next step is to import the dataset. For this exercise, we are using the Advertising dataset, which is available for download at https://www.kaggle.com/fayomi/advertising/data/. The dataset was created by Udemy course instructor Jose Portilla of Pierian Data and is used in his course *Python for Data Science and Machine Learning Bootcamp*.

Import the dataset with the `pd.read_csv` command into a Pandas dataframe and preview the dataframe using the `head` command.

```
df = pd.read_csv('~/Downloads/advertising.csv')
```

```
df.head()
```

```
1  import pandas as pd
2  from sklearn.naive_bayes import GaussianNB
3
4  df = pd.read_csv('~/Downloads/advertising.csv')
5
6  df.head()
7
```

	Daily Time Spent on Site	Age	Area Income	Daily Internet Usage	Ad Topic Line	City	Male	Country	Timestamp	Clicked on Ad
0	68.95	35	61833.90	256.09	Cloned 5thgeneration orchestration	Wrightburgh	0	Tunisia	2016-03-27 00:53:11	0
1	80.23	31	68441.85	193.77	Monitored national standardization	West Jodi	1	Nauru	2016-04-04 01:39:02	0
2	69.47	26	59785.94	236.50	Organic bottom-line service-desk	Davidton	0	San Marino	2016-03-13 20:35:42	0
3	74.15	29	54806.18	245.89	Triple-buffered reciprocal time-frame	West Terrifurt	1	Italy	2016-01-10 02:31:19	0
4	68.37	35	73889.99	225.58	Robust logistical utilization	South Manuel	0	Iceland	2016-06-03 03:36:18	0

Step 3

Next, let's remove discrete variables from the dataset using the delete method and inputting the names of the columns we wish to remove. (Our chosen algorithm only accepts continuous variables as independent variables.[15])

```
del df['Ad Topic Line']

del df['Timestamp']

del df['City']

del df['Country']

del df['Male']
```

---

[15] Continuous variables are infinite and compatible with mathematical operations such as addition, subtraction, division, etc. Numeric variables, including integers and floating-point numbers, are therefore considered continuous as they can be aggregated or manipulated as natural numbers. Discrete variables, meanwhile are variables of a finite value and cannot be aggregated or mathematically manipulated with other variable observations. Examples include city of residence and gender (as there is generally only one acceptable value).

71

Step 4

Let's now assign our X (independent variables) values and y value (dependent variable). The y variable is "Clicked On Ad" and the X variables consist of the remaining variables (Age, Area Income, Daily Internet Usage, and Daily Time Spent on Site).

Please note that in data science the lower case "y" and upper case "X" are standard conventions for denoting the dependent variable and independent variables respectively.

```
#Assign all columns in the dataset as X variables, excluding
"Clicked On Ad"
X = df.drop('Clicked on Ad',axis=1)
```

```
#Assign "Clicked on Ad" as y variable
y = df['Clicked on Ad']
```

Step 5

We now want to assign our X and y variables to the Gaussian Naive Bayes algorithm from Scikit-learn. Gaussian is the easiest and simplest version of this algorithm. It is used with continuous variables under the assumption of normal data distribution. The Bernoulli version of Naive Bayes, meanwhile, is a more suitable classification technique for use with multiple binary features. For more information regarding specific algorithms for Naive Bayes classification, please see: https://scikit-learn.org/stable/modules/classes.html#module-sklearn.naive_bayes

We also need to assign a variable to the algorithm, which in this case is `model`. The naming of the variable isn't important as long as it's an intuitive description and fits with the basic syntax for assigning variables in Python (i.e. no spaces, cannot begin with a number, etc.).

```
model = GaussianNB()
```

Next, we need to fit the algorithm to our X and y data using the assigned variable name.

```
model.fit(X, y)
```

Step 6

The final step is to input the values of a sample user that we wish to test.

Feature	Target Value
Daily Time Spent on Site	66.00
Age	48
Area Income	24593.33
Daily Internet Usage	131.76

Table 6: Target user information

```
target_user = [

        66.00, #Daily Time Spent on Site

        48, #Age

        24593.33, #Area Income

        131.76, #Daily Internet Usage

]
```

Lastly, apply the `predict` method to the `target_user` using the model developed in Step 5 and assign it as a new variable. Then `print` the new variable on a new line.

```
pred_target_user = model.predict([target_user])
print("Prediction:", pred_target_user)
```

Let's run the model by right-clicking and selecting "Run" or by navigating from the Jupyter Notebook menu to Cell > Run All. Wait one or two seconds for the computer to process the model. The results, as shown below, will then appear at the bottom of the cell.

```
Prediction: [1]
```

The outcome of this exercise for the y variable "Clicked on Ad" is [1], which means that the target user is expected to click on the advertisement and the ad should therefore be recommended to this user. Conversely, an outcome of [0] signifies that the user *is not* expected to click on the advertisement based on the behavior of similar users.

A more advanced version of this exercise examining both discrete and continuous variables (using logistic regression) is available at:

http://www.scatterplotpress.com/bonus-chapters/recommender-systems-for-absolute-

beginners-chapter-7/

8

CONTENT-BASED FILTERING

As established in Chapter 2, content-based filtering methods provide recommendations based on similar item attributes and the profile of an individual user's preferences. The content-based filtering system then attempts to recommend items similar to those that a user has liked or browsed in the past. After purchasing a book about "machine learning," for example, Amazon's content-based filtering is likely to serve you other books:

- from the same author,

- from the same category, e.g., data science, and

- have similar title keywords, e.g., "machine learning."

As expected, content-based filtering relies heavily on a description of the item's characteristics and the profiling of individual user preferences. Under this model, items such as documents, online posts, images, and videos need to be adequately described in the form of keywords/tagging/metadata or through more sophisticated methods such as image recognition (e.g., artificial neural networks) or text mining (e.g., TF.IDF).

A book, for example, could be described by the following metadata:

1. The author(s)
2. The genre, e.g., thriller, romantic, statistics & probability
3. The year of publication
4. The type of book, e.g., fiction, non-fiction
5. Book format, e.g., textbook, audiobook, e-book, hardcopy

Likewise, user preferences need to be known and recorded. Individual user preferences' can be determined by examining:

1. Past purchasing/consumption behavior
2. Browsing history
3. Personal details, e.g., gender, location, nationality, and hobbies
4. The IP address to determine location and time zone

From information gleaned about the user, filtering techniques can then compare this data with the description of available items and identify items to recommend. Content-based filtering can be a highly effective approach given that the items are properly tagged and there's sufficient data about the user.

Advantages

1) Agnostic to crowd preferences

A major advantage of content-based filtering is that it aids the discovery of relevant but low-profile items. As content-based filtering doesn't take crowd preferences into account, relevant items with low exposure to the crowd can still be found.

2) Content items are stable

Items don't change over time as much as people and are generally more permanent. People, on the other hand, are fickle and our tastes change dramatically over time. We're all guilty of following phases of consumption. But, an item will always be an item, and content-based filtering is therefore less vulnerable (than collaborative filtering) to changes in crowd preferences.

3) Items are generally fewer than users

Most online platforms have fewer items than users, and content-based filtering can help to conserve computational resources by comparing a limited number of items rather than a larger volume of user relationships.

4) Compatible with new items

In cases where there are insufficient rating data for a new or existing item (cold-start), content filtering can be applied to gather information regarding other items rated/purchased/consumed by the target user that might share similar attributes. The item is therefore recommended based on the user's interaction with similar items despite the lack of direct historical data.

5) Mitigates cheating

The other notable benefit of content filtering is that it's generally more difficult to "game the system" because malicious actors have less control to manipulate or fabricate item-to-item relationships. This is not the case for item-to-user relationships, which can be easily inflated with a flood of fake positive reviews and purchases.

Disadvantages

1) Low variety

The variety of recommended items can be limited and less diverse than other methods. This is because content-based filtering depends on matching a specific item with similar items. Thus, items with low to no exposure to the target user are not likely to surface, which limits item discoverability.

2) Ineffective for new users

While content-based filtering methods excel at recommending new items, this isn't the case for new users. Without information about the user's preferences to construct a user profile, there's little way of recommending related items. To mitigate the cold-start problem, online platforms may attempt to extract relevant keywords when onboarding new users using a knowledge-based approach. Pinterest, for example, directs new users to specify a collection of over-arching interests that are used to establish a preliminary user profile and match item descriptions to content recommendations. Pinterest's machine learning-based algorithms then refine the user's profile and their specific interests based on observing their "pins" and browsing behavior.

3) Mixed quality of results

Content-based filtering is generally accurate at selecting relevant items, but the quality of such items can sometimes be poor. As content-based filtering ignores the item ratings of other users, they are limited by their ability to decipher the quality of an item.

Exercise: Recommending real estate properties

For our third and final exercise, we will use the nearest neighbors algorithm to identify relevant real estate recommendations for properties in Melbourne, Australia. The recommendations will be generated based on the user's previous search behavior on an online real estate portal where we know that the user is interested in houses located in Melbourne, Australia with these seven feature values:

Price: $1,350,000 AUD

Distance to the city: 2km

Bedrooms: 2

Bathrooms: 2

Land size: 220m²

Building size: 200m²

Year built: 2005

Using the nearest neighbors algorithm as a content-based filtering technique, we want to find three property listings with similar specifications. The three properties deemed most similar to the user's known preference will then be sent to the user as part of a promotional email campaign.

About Nearest Neighbors

Nearest neighbors is a simple clustering technique that creates clusters based on the closest distance between data points. Using this technique, we find the shortest distance between two data points and fuse them into one cluster. This step is repeated so that the next shortest distance between two data points is found, which either expands the size of the first cluster or forms a new cluster between two individual data points. For this exercise, we are searching for the closest three data points to a specified data point, which is determined by the user's earlier search query.

Step 1

The first step is to install our libraries. For this exercise, we need to import Pandas and Scikit-learn's nearest neighbors algorithm.

```
import pandas as pd
from sklearn.neighbors import NearestNeighbors
```

Step 2

The next step is to import the dataset into Jupyter Notebook using `pd.read_csv`. The dataset is called Melbourne_housing_FULL and should be first downloaded and unzipped from https://www.kaggle.com/anthonypino/melbourne-housing-market/.

```
df = pd.read_csv('~/Downloads/Melbourne_housing_FULL.csv')
```

This command will load the data into a Pandas dataframe, and we can use the `head` command to preview the dataset inside Jupyter Notebook.

```
df.head()
```

```
1  import pandas as pd
2  from sklearn.neighbors import NearestNeighbors
3
4  df = pd.read_csv('~/Downloads/Melbourne_housing_FULL.csv')
5
6  df.head()
7
```

	Suburb	Address	Rooms	Type	Price	Method	SellerG	Date	Distance	Postcode	...	Bathroom	Car
0	Abbotsford	68 Studley St	2	h	NaN	SS	Jellis	3/09/2016	2.5	3067.0	...	1.0	1.0
1	Abbotsford	85 Turner St	2	h	1480000.0	S	Biggin	3/12/2016	2.5	3067.0	...	1.0	1.0
2	Abbotsford	25 Bloomburg St	2	h	1035000.0	S	Biggin	4/02/2016	2.5	3067.0	...	1.0	0.0
3	Abbotsford	18/659 Victoria St	3	u	NaN	VB	Rounds	4/02/2016	2.5	3067.0	...	2.0	1.0
4	Abbotsford	5 Charles St	3	h	1465000.0	SP	Biggin	4/03/2017	2.5	3067.0	...	2.0	0.0

5 rows × 21 columns

Step 3

Next, drop rows with missing values using the `dropna` command. (Missing values cannot be used with this algorithm).

```
df.dropna(axis = 0, how = 'any', thresh = None, subset = None,
inplace = True)
```

An `axis` argument of "0" drops rows with missing values, whereas an argument of "1" drops columns with missing values.

Documentation: http://bit.ly/2KqV1a7

Step 4

The fourth step is to specify the columns that we wish to examine as input features, which must be continuous (floating-point or integer values) such as the number of bathrooms (e.g., 2) and land size (e.g., 245.5). This means we can't include string values such as property type (e.g., house, apartment) or address (e.g., 25 Bloomburg st) as these variables are discrete.

Below are all the features contained in the Melbourne housing dataset as well as their feature class. The highlighted features are those chosen for our sample model.

Feature	Feature Class	Feature	Feature Class
Suburb	String	Bedroom2	Integer
Address	String	Bathroom	Integer
Rooms	Integer	Car	Integer
Type	String	Landsize	Integer
Price	Integer	BuildingArea	Integer
Method	String	YearBuilt	Integer
SellerG	String	CouncilArea	String
Date	TimeDate	Latitude	String
Distance	Float	Longitude	String
Postcode	Integer	Regionname	String
Propertycount	Integer		

Table 7: Feature information from the Melbourne Housing dataset

```
#Specify included features

X = df.loc[:, ['Price', 'Distance', 'Bedroom2', 'Bathroom',

'Landsize', 'BuildingArea', 'YearBuilt']].values
```

Step 5

Next, input the values of our target as listed in the following table.

Feature	Target Value
Price	$1,350,000
Distance to the City	2km
Bedrooms	2
Bathrooms	2
Land Size	220m^2
Building Size	200m^2
Year Built	2005

Table 8: Known preferences of the target user based on their search history

```
#Specify target values

target = [1350000, 2, 2, 2, 220, 200, 2005]
```

Step 6

Let's now create a new variable to `fit` the nearest neighbors algorithm to `X` and specify the number of neighbors as 3.

```
model = NearestNeighbors(n_neighbors = 3).fit(X)
```

Step 7

The final step is to `print` the nearest neighbors of the target data point using the model developed in Step 6.

```
print(model.kneighbors([target]))
```

Click "Run" or navigate to Cell > Run All from the top menu. By clicking "Run," the model will find the three data points that are most quantitatively similar to the target data point. The results are as follows:

```
(array([[11.71537451, 17.12191578, 46.64643609]]), array([[6, 3002, 6669]]))
```

The first array contains the distance from the target point to each neighbor, while the second array contains the corresponding row position of each neighbor. With the arrays sequenced in descending order, we can see that the row at position 6 is the closest to the target data point at 11.71537451, while the row at position 6669 is the third furthest neighbor at 46.64643609. Thus, if we were to modify our algorithm to select the two closest neighbors, the model would return rows 6 and 3002.

To find the house properties position at 6, 3002, and 6669, we can use the df.iloc[] command as demonstrated.

```
#Find row 6

df.iloc[6]
```

```
Suburb                        Abbotsford
Address                  40 Nicholson St
Rooms                                  3
Type                                   h
Price                           1.35e+06
Method                                VB
SellerG                           Nelson
Date                          12/11/2016
Distance                             2.5
Postcode                            3067
Bedroom2                               3
Bathroom                               2
Car                                    2
Landsize                             214
BuildingArea                         190
YearBuilt                           2005
CouncilArea                        Yarra
Lattitude                       -37.8085
Longtitude                       144.996
Regionname        Northern Metropolitan
Propertycount                       4019
```

```
#Find row 3002

df.iloc[3002]
```

```
Suburb                              Seddon
Address                        38 Lily St
Rooms                                    3
Type                                     h
Price                             1.35e+06
Method                                  PI
SellerG                            Village
Date                             8/10/2016
Distance                               6.6
Postcode                              3011
Bedroom2                                 3
Bathroom                                 3
Car                                      2
Landsize                               227
BuildingArea                           211
YearBuilt                             2015
CouncilArea      Maribyrnong City Council
Lattitude                         -37.8033
Longtitude                         144.89
Regionname           Western Metropolitan
Propertycount                         2417
```

#Find row 6669

df.iloc[6669]

```
Suburb                             Northcote
Address                      39 Winifred St
Rooms                                      4
Type                                       h
Price                               1.35e+06
Method                                     S
SellerG                                  Ray
Date                              23/09/2017
Distance                                 5.3
Postcode                                3070
Bedroom2                                   4
Bathroom                                   2
Car                                        2
Landsize                                 264
BuildingArea                             188
YearBuilt                               1996
CouncilArea        Darebin City Council
Lattitude                           -37.769
Longtitude                          144.986
Regionname         Northern Metropolitan
Propertycount                          11364
```

We have now identified the three properties most similar to the user's known preference, which are located in the suburbs of

Abbotsford, Seddon, and Northcote respectively. To entice the user to return to our online portal, we can email these three property listings from our dataset as content recommendations to the user.

EVALUATION

If you're familiar with the mechanics of machine learning, you might have noticed the absence of training and test data in the models used in the exercises thus far. An explanation for this vital question will be revealed later in this chapter, but, first, let's review the rationale of split validation.

The partition of a dataset into training data and test data, known as split validation, is a fundamental part of machine learning. The training data is used to detect general patterns and design a prediction model, while the test data is used to road test the model and compare the results. Thus, if we reserve 30% of the data and test it with the model developed from patterns discovered in the initial 70% of the data, will the model's predictions still hold accurate?

Two possible reasons why the model may falter at making predictions using the test data are overfitting and underfitting. Overfitting exists when the model adjusts itself to fit patterns in the training data but is too rigid to then replicate the same level of accuracy with new test data. Underfitting, meanwhile, is where the model is overly simple and is a weak predictor of the test data.

There are numerous techniques to compare the performance of the model using the training data and the test data. For classification-based models, a popular method is the confusion matrix, which is a simple table that tabulates the performance of classification algorithms such as Naive Bayes Classifier and logistic regression.

	Predicted 0	Predicted 1
Actual is 0	Correct	Incorrect
Actual is 1	Incorrect	Correct

Table 9: Confusion matrix

In Table 10, there are a total of 105 data points in the dataset. As highlighted diagonally below, the model predicted 50 data points correctly as "0" and 48 cases as "1".

	Predicted 0	Predicted 1
Actual is 0	50	5
Actual is 1	2	48

Table 10: Results added to the confusion matrix

Meanwhile, the same model incorrectly predicted five data points as "1" and two data points as "0". This means that five data points were classified as "1", when in fact they should've been classified as "0" (false-positive), and two data points were predicted to be "0" but should have been classified as "1" (false-negative). Reviewing the results of the confusion matrix for the training and test datasets can then be used to make comparisons regarding prediction performance.

Coding Example

Below is a code example of the same Bayes' model used to recommend online advertisements in Chapter 7, but, this time, using split validation and a confusion matrix to analyze prediction accuracy.

```
#Import libraries
import pandas as pd
from sklearn.naive_bayes import GaussianNB
from sklearn.model_selection import train_test_split
from sklearn.metrics import classification_report,
confusion_matrix

#Import dataset
df = pd.read_csv('~/Downloads/advertising.csv')
```

```python
#Delete variables
del df['Ad Topic Line']
del df['Timestamp']
del df['City']
del df['Male']
del df ['Country']


#Assign X and y variables
X = df.drop('Clicked on Ad',axis=1)
y = df['Clicked on Ad']


# Split the data into training and test tests (70/30)
X_train, X_test, y_train, y_test = train_test_split(X, y,
test_size=0.3, random_state=10)


#Assign model
model = GaussianNB()


#Fit the algorithm to the training data
model.fit(X_train, y_train)


# Assign a new variable to the prediction of the X test data
model_predict = model.predict(X_test)


#Confusion matrix
```

```
print(confusion_matrix(y_test, model_predict))
```

```
 1  #Import libraries
 2  import pandas as pd
 3  from sklearn.naive_bayes import GaussianNB
 4  from sklearn.model_selection import train_test_split
 5  from sklearn.metrics import classification_report, confusion_matrix
 6
 7  #Import dataset
 8  df = pd.read_csv('~/Downloads/advertising.csv')
 9
10  #Delete variables
11  del df['Ad Topic Line']
12  del df['Timestamp']
13  del df['City']
14  del df['Male']
15  del df ['Country']
16
17  #Assign X and y variables
18  X = df.drop('Clicked on Ad',axis=1)
19  y = df['Clicked on Ad']
20
21  #Split the data into training and test tests
22  X_train, X_test, y_train, y_test = train_test_split(X, y, test_size=0.3, random_state=10)
23
24  #Assign model
25  model = GaussianNB()
26
27  #Fit the algorithm to the training data
28  model.fit(X_train, y_train)
29
30  # Assign a new variable to the prediction of the X test data
31  model_predict = model.predict(X_test)
32
33  #Confusion matrix
34  print(confusion_matrix(y_test, model_predict))
35
```

```
[[138   8]
 [  6 148]]
```

In this example, the model has recorded just 8 false-positives and 6 false-negatives among 300 cases.

Other Methods

Other methods of evaluation used in conjunction with split validation are root mean square error (RMSE) and mean absolute error (MAE), which are used for numeric predictions rather than classification problems.

In the case of RMSE, the process starts by taking a subset of user ratings (i.e., 80%) as the training set, designing a recommender system based on that data and then using that model to predict the ratings of the remaining (20% of) users with the test set. Subsequently, you might discover that a user rated an item 5-stars but the model predicted 3.5 stars. The error here is 1.5 stars. Using RMSE, you can then compute the average of the errors and generate a final error rate.

Mean absolute error, meanwhile, is less sensitive to large errors and doesn't penalize poor predictions as heavily as RMSE. As an example, if the model regularly predicted 5-stars and the actual user rating was 1-star, then the final error score would not be as high as the equivalent RMSE error score. In the case of the famous Netflix Prize launched in 2007, teams were handed a training and test set of real user ratings, and their target was to achieve RMSE of less than 10%.

However, more than a decade on, the currency of offline methods including RMSE, MAE, the confusion matrix, and split validation (training and test data) has depreciated. While these methods are used still for internal feedback prior to production and for academic research, the industry has drifted away from pure machine learning and the credo of split validation. Internet companies and recommender system specialists have instead shifted their attention to online evaluation methods such as A/B testing, click-through-rate (CTR), and ROI (return on investment) metrics as well as qualitative research.

Although statistically sound in its approach, split validation encounters significant problems when met with the realities of human interaction. While a confusion matrix is effective at comparing the results of the training and test data in an offline environment, numerous real-world factors cause the model to unravel when put into operation.

Recommending items highly correlated to a target user who is already familiar with a proposed combination of movies, such as those of the Harry Potter or Star Wars series, can be redundant. This problem is exacerbated if closely related items—such as those of the same series—are displayed in another tab adjacent to the recommended items section. If users become accustomed to seeing the same popular and obvious recommendations in their sidebar, they will gradually lose interest. An element of serendipity is a major advantage of recommender systems. Therefore, a slightly lower correlation between items might provide more effective recommendations and a higher conversion rate.

The effectiveness of recommendations also varies by use case and how recommendations are displayed. Highly correlated item recommendations may perform poorly on the home page but enjoy a higher conversion rate when placed deeper into the website. A key goal of recommender systems is item discovery, and it may take several instances of exposure before the user is ready to purchase or complete a target conversion action. This is why some Internet companies follow a policy of cycling recommendations to users three or more times before determining whether the suggested item is a poor match.

Thus, while the training and test data split may be a convenient method to evaluate the data scientist's technical abilities, it does little to assess the final performance of a system intended for use in the real world and managing factors outside the model's initial consideration.

The interpretation of the results can also differ by organization. Monetized blogs that generate revenue based on page views and ad impressions may not be affected by a high exit rate from recommended content. Alternatively, businesses that focus on content marketing to build rapport with their customers and improve their search engine rankings might not be satisfied with a recommender system that leads to a shallow level of user engagement.

Most exponents of recommender systems, therefore, evaluate model performance based on customized user actions rather than split validation. One method is user studies, which involves observing how users interact with recommender systems via online screen recordings or experimental trials. Meanwhile, more large-scale evaluations can be performed with the aid of A/B testing.

A/B Testing

In A/B testing, two prediction models randomly alternate between users so comparisons can be formed from the results of Group A and Group B. Users in Group A might be fed collaborative-based filtering recommendations, while users in Group B might be exposed to content-based recommendations.

A/B tests typically require a thousand or more users to accurately assess the performance of one recommender system model over another. The performance of the systems can be evaluated based on numerous metrics. A primary metric is analyzing the click-through rate of items recommended to the user (usually displayed inside the website's sidebar or below a post). Recommended items that generate a high-click rate are looked upon favorably. A/B testing can also be implemented in the design and labeling of recommended items. A/B tests, however, should only test one variable at a time.

To ensure that the model is effective at maximizing user engagement, A/B testing may also need to factor in time-on-page or the exit rate of users who click through to a recommended item. If a user immediately exits after arriving on the page of a recommended item, this is unlikely to be considered a positive result.

A/B testing, itself, can be performed in a variety of ways and there are numerous SaaS (software-as-a-service) options available, including Optimizely and VWO.

The advantages of A/B testing over user studies are scalability and relevance. Through automation, A/B testing can be scaled out to thousands or even millions of users, albeit at some extra cost. Secondly, A/B test results are highly relevant as they capture genuine interactions between the end-user and the recommended item(s). Users are generally impervious to the fact that a website is conducting live A/B testing and aren't coerced to select a recommended item as they might in a user study.

User Studies

While user studies are more difficult to scale and generate results in a contrived environment, they do generate valuable qualitative insights. Rather than solely looking at the numbers—as is the case with A/B testing—user studies may elicit ideas and feedback to optimize the recommender system and its interface.

For instance, feedback might comprise suggestions that the recommended items were too similar to items the user had already purchased or consumed in the past. Rather than being recommended a near-identical item, perhaps, the user prefers some variety in their recommendations. Users might also offer feedback that they prefer not to watch back-to-back-to-back videos of cats swinging around the room on a fan because it makes them feel nauseous and the entertainment factor has a diminishing rate of return. Instead, they'd prefer to switch up their viewing activity with tips on cat grooming and highlights of cats performing other spectacular feats. User studies can also help provide specific feedback on the visual design and labeling of recommender systems.

While it's hazardous to redo your entire recommender system based on qualitative feedback from a small number of users, user study suggestions can be tested and validated using A/B testing. A combination of user studies and A/B testing is indeed an ideal evaluation strategy.

Lastly, qualitative feedback can be valuable in highlighting aspects overlooked in an A/B test. Speaking on the re-installment of Netflix's online subscriber profile feature, former Chief Product Officer, Neil Hunt, told CNNMoney, "focus-group testing showed that profiles generate more viewing and more engagement."

The subscriber profile feature allows a single paid subscriber account to manage multiple individual users (e.g., husband and wife, two roommates) with separate user features including ratings and friend lists to produce tailored recommendations.

"Listening to our members, we realized that users of this feature often describe it as an essential part of their Netflix experience," explained Hunt.

This particular example underlines the importance of qualitative feedback in a quantitative-centric era of doing business.

In conclusion, when it comes to recommender systems, evaluation can be messy. Also, the more you look at the results post-implementation, the more feedback and suggestions for optimization you will find. Recommender systems, therefore sit on the edge of machine learning and their own specialized subfield. They employ the same algorithms and self-learning techniques as other machine learning applications but rely on their own methods of evaluation outside of split validation and other traditional performance metrics.

The complexity of recommender model evaluation also means that there are ample jobs, prize money, and engaging work for those looking to build their career in this breakaway subfield of machine learning.

10

PRIVACY & ETHICS

As previously stated, recommender systems can be incredibly powerful predictors of people's likes and dislikes. Their reliance on implicit and explicit user feedback helps to identify unique user preferences, but in doing so, reveals relevant information about a person's political views, health condition, sexual orientation, and other private information. In some cases, the information collected and processed is benign, e.g., a user's preferred Internet browser, but other times, information can be highly sensitive and provoke concerns regarding personal privacy. Users searching for sensitive content such as personal well-being, health and relationship advice might not feel comfortable browsing platforms that repurpose their behavior to produce recommendations. There is a danger that these preferences could be later revealed to friends, colleagues, classmates, and family from content and ads displayed on their screen.

In 2009, a woman in America's Midwest sued Netflix after her sexual preferences were disclosed online. Using the pseudonym "Doe", the Netflix user sued the company for including her personal information in the 2007 Netflix Prize dataset. The lawsuit was filed after academic research at the University of

Texas demonstrated privacy flaws in the design of the dataset Netflix used for the competition.

Despite Netflix's attempt to remove personal identifiers from the data, including the names of individuals, the identities were revealed by matching the competition's dataset with film ratings from the publicly available Internet Movie Database. The researchers found that an anonymous user's rating of six obscure movies could be used to identify an individual Netflix user with an 84% success rate.[16] Moreover, the accuracy rate rose to 99% when the date of a movie review was known.[17]

In the case of Doe vs Netflix, the latter was ruled to have violated U.S. Fair Trade laws and the Video Privacy Protection Act. The ongoing lawsuit also led Netflix to cancel the second Netflix Prize competition planned for 2010.

Although open data competitions and recommender systems have continued to develop and expand, data privacy remains a highly sensitive issue. In April 2018, Facebook Founder Mark Zuckerberg testified before Congress regarding his company's sharing policies of user data. His appearance at Capitol Hill was part of a hearing into Facebook's sharing of voter preferences with a data analysis firm that allegedly provided support to the Donald Trump election campaign.

---

[16] Viktor Mayer-Schonberger & Kenneth Cukier, "Big Data: A Revolution That Will Transform How We Live, Work and Think," *Hodder & Stoughton*, 2013.
[17] Viktor Mayer-Schonberger & Kenneth Cukier, "Big Data: A Revolution That Will Transform How We Live, Work and Think," *Hodder & Stoughton*, 2013.

While the Facebook and Netflix examples both highlight concerns over the management of user data rather than the use of specific algorithms (such as those explored in this book), the current socio-political environment has repercussions on the use of recommender systems. The scrutiny surrounding data privacy is significant because user data is used to feed personalized recommender systems. The availability of real data for open competitions is also vital for the development of the industry and the advancement of algorithm-based models, as was the intention of the first Netflix Prize.

New regulations, though, are set to have a major impact on organizations that collect and store user data. This includes Europe's new online data privacy law known as GDPR. The new law introduces added transparency for users regarding how their data is processed and the use of cookies on web applications, as well as a clarified "right to be forgotten" when users no longer wish their data to be retained (given there are no legitimate grounds for keeping it). GDPR also requires the encryption of users' stored personal data and the right of users to accept or reject the use of their personal information for the application of online recommendations.

Beyond the issues of data availability and transparency, there are also specific concerns about the use of recommender systems. Based on recent regulatory changes in Europe, hearings by Congress in the United States, and tweets from Donald Trump, governments are undeniably concerned about the growing threat of online content manipulation. This includes biased content delivery, attempts by state-backed organizations to manipulate public sentiment through paid advertising, and the projection of fake news on online platforms.

All three concerns have a direct relationship with content-feeding algorithms and the platforms that design these content display systems. The algorithms that feed content to users on Facebook, for example, have little way of weeding out fake stories from genuine news stories or the ability to remain bipartisan in the case of a political election. While measures can be made to block known sources of false information, little can be done to halt the biases that inherently emerge from user-collected data, short of avoiding these systems altogether.

For some companies, such as Napster, avoidance may prove the only option. Despite calls for the file-sharing site to harness its access to personal information (on upwards of 70 million users) to recommend music to users and aid the discovery of lesser-known artists, the company's management and legal advisors ruled against the proposal.[18] The implementation of collaborative filtering—as proposed by music enthusiasts working at Napster as computer engineers—would have reinforced claims from the record labels that the platform was directing users to pirated

---

[18] Joseph Menn, "All the Rave: The Rise and Fall of Shawn Fanning's Napster," *Joseph Menn*, First Edition, 2011.

content. Like telecommunication companies refusing to take responsibility for illegal activities conducted on their infrastructure, Napster chose to distance itself from any form of user misdoings on their platform.[19] Napster maintained that it was strictly a platform, and, thus, could not take responsibility for the actions of its users. While this decision didn't impede lawsuits and the eventual demise of Napster's original service, it highlights the legal risk of implementing recommender systems and especially collaborative filtering.

Whether driven by fear of legal retribution or by more altruistic motives, it's essential for all organizations that engage in personalized recommender systems to outline and agree to a general code of ethics and compliance. This includes compliance with the laws and regulations in the countries and regions they operate and where data is stored. Under China's new Cybersecurity Law, for example, Chinese citizens' personal data collected in Mainland China cannot be moved and stored outside the Mainland.

Amidst the current backdrop, the US National Academies are proposing a data science oath, including commitments that "I will respect the privacy of my data subjects", and "I will remember that my data are not just data numbers without meaning or context, but represent real people and situations and that my

---

[19] Joseph Menn, "All the Rave: The Rise and Fall of Shawn Fanning's Napster," *Joseph Menn,* First Edition, 2011.

work may lead to unintended societal consequences."[20] Other principles advocated for by the data science ethics community are consideration of consent, alertness to bias, and protecting data from becoming deanonymized.

A practical first step for organizations that wish to minimize legal risk and other public repercussions is to scrutinize what information is added to the recommendation engine in the first place. While there's limited capacity to control the output of model-based predictions, steps can be taken to limit the scope of data variables chosen for filtering. This may mean removing sensitive variables such as "marital status" and "race" to predict the suitability of credit card applicants or the display of online advertisements.

In addition, it's important to encourage transparency internally and ensure that relevant departments such as upper management and legal teams are aware of the variables chosen to generate recommendations as well as the composition of what is recommended to users as output. The latter is especially important given the growing scrutiny of what online platforms recommend to users.

One of these concerned voices is Zeynep Tufekci, an associate professor at the School of Information and Library Science at the University of North Carolina, who has publicized YouTube's

---

[20] Robert Langkjaer-Bain in Significance, "Data Rights and Wrongs," *Royal Statistical Society*, Volume 15, Issue 6, 2018.

proclivity to push users toward extreme content through its autoplay recommendation algorithm. Published in a *New York Times* article in early 2018, Tufekci documented how YouTube led her to white supremacist rants, Holocaust denials and other disturbing content following the viewing of Donald Trump rallies on the platform.[21] Similarly, viewership of Hillary Clinton and Bernie Sanders' videos—using a newly created YouTube account—led Tufekci to videos conspiratorial in nature, including the existence of secret government agencies and alleged involvement in the September 11 attacks by the U.S. government. In both cases, YouTube recommended content progressively more extreme over the course of Tufekci's user journey and to content radically less mainstream in opinion than her original search.

Former Google engineer Guillaume Chaslot is vocal as well in questioning the ethics of the parent company. While at Google, Chaslot worked in a team developing recommendation algorithms for YouTube. Chaslot points to what he calls a bias towards anti-media content and a recommender system that amplifies resentment against other media sources.[22] During the 2016 U.S. election, Chaslot noticed candidates most aggressive against the

---

[21] Zeynep Tufekci, "YouTube, the Great Radicalizer", *New York Times*, accessed April 11, 2018, https://www.nytimes.com/2018/03/10/opinion/sunday/youtube-politics-radical.html/.

[22] Guillaume Chaslot, "How Algorithms Can Learn to Discredit the Media," *Medium*, accessed April 11, 2018, https://medium.com/@guillaumechaslot/how-algorithms-can-learn-to-discredit-the-media-d1360157c4fa/.

media were recommended by YouTube four times more frequently than their opponents.[23]

Chaslot has also spearheaded the launch of a website called algotransparency.org that includes research tools to inform the public about what drives recommender algorithms, such as those used by YouTube.[24] Tracked content topics include political elections, mass shootings, and science—and even the question of whether the earth is flat. Needless to say, the debate around the ethical impact of recommender technology will remain a hot topic in the years to come and should be a top-level consideration for data scientists and companies.

Another major priority for the industry is upholding the trust of end-users. In countries and regions where there's an established culture around data privacy, user trust can be preserved by offering users a clause to opt-out from using their personal information for predictive filtering. Trust can also be boosted through transparency and disclaimers on how and why the site delivers recommendations to its users.

Part of the practice of transparency lies in the labeling of recommended content. In the 2013 research paper *Sponsored vs. Organic Recommendations and the Impact of Labeling*, researchers in Germany found that the labeling technique of

---

[23] Guillaume Chaslot, "YouTube's A.I. was divisive in the US presidential election," *Medium,* accessed April 11, 2018, https://medium.com/the-graph/youtubes-ai-is-neutral-towards-clicks-but-is-biased-towards-people-and-ideas-3a2f643dea9a/.
[24] The site currently only examines YouTube but is expected to add tools to track other online platforms in the future.

recommended items significantly impacted users' reactions.[25] The study found that the click-through rate for recommended content labeled as "Sponsored" was 5.93% but was 8.86% when the same content was labeled as "Organic." Content without a label performed attracted a click-through rate of 9.87%.

This research indicates that it's not necessarily in the best interest of online platforms, or advertisers, to label recommended content. However, the exact click-through and response rate of labeled item recommendations will vary across platforms and use cases. Some platforms embrace transparency to their advantage. This includes Spotify, whose users are partly drawn to the service by the knowledge that other users' tastes assist in the discovery of music.

In conclusion, the sensitivity of recommender systems can range from benign and inconsequential to legally unsafe and damaging to the long-term success of an organization. Understanding where your recommender engine sits on the spectrum of potential legal retribution and impact on users' trust is essential. The answer will depend heavily on what data variables you choose to collect and process, how you store and use that information, what level of operational transparency you provide

---

[25] Joeran Beel, Stefan Langer & Marcel Genzmehr, "Sponsored vs. Organic Recommendations and the Impact of Labeling," in Trond Aalberg; Milena Dobreva; Christos Papatheodorou; Giannis Tsakonas; Charles Farrugia, *Proceedings of the 17th International Conference on Theory and Practice of Digital Libraries (TPDL 2013)*. pp. 395–399, September 2013.

internally and what you decide to disclose externally to your end-users.

11

THE FUTURE OF RECOMMENDER SYSTEMS

Recommender systems are one of the most visible applications of machine learning and data mining today, and their uncanny ability to convert our unspoken actions into presenting items we desire and accept is both addictive and concerning. Cloudera Founder Jeffrey Hammerbache laments "the best minds of my generation are thinking about how to make people click ads,"[26] and Ex-Google employee Seth Stephens-Davidowitz envisages that "all the next Newton's and Freud's will be data scientists."[27] It's also difficult to foresee government intervention slowing down the sophistication of recommender systems and especially given that so many end-users are willing to volunteer personal information to online platforms in exchange for access to their services.

---

[26] Drake Baer, "Why Data God Jeffrey Hammerbacher Left Facebook To Found Cloudera," *Fast Company*, accessed April 20, 2018, https://www.fastcompany.com/3008436/why-data-god-jeffrey-hammerbacher-left-facebook-found-cloudera/.
[27] Seth Stephens-Davidowitz, "Everybody Lies: Big Data, New Data, and What the Internet Can Tell Us About Who We Really Are," *Dey Street Books*, 2017.

In this final chapter, we take a look at the coming developments in recommender system technology and architecture.

Audio Content Mining

With the recent explosion of audio content from podcasts and audiobooks, there are various opportunities in voice recognition, dictation, and natural language processing (NLP). This is especially so given that podcasts are a fertile medium for books, products, films, services, and other podcast series recommendations. Given that podcast listeners generally consume content on the go or while multi-tasking, a system to link book and product recommendations made by their trusted podcast hosts to a more convenient setting such as Amazon could also be highly lucrative. Audio content is also a great medium to build demographic profiles of users, such as sports fans, self-help enthusiasts, travel lovers, and computer programmers.

One technique that can be used to extract data from audio content is named entity recognition. As a vital tool in the NLP toolbox, named entity recognition picks out salient parts of text or speech such as *what (Stata Data Conference)*, *where (New York)*, and *who (data scientists)*. This extracted data can then be used as input data to feed knowledge-based, demographic or content-based recommendations to users.

However, due to the inherent difficulties in decoding audio content into topics and conducting named entity recognition or sentiment analysis, podcasts have not undergone the same intense "recommendization" as text-based content or even video content.

Tech writer Elliot Zaagman suggests that the answer could lie in part with Apple's identity and focus on hardware rather than content aggregation. As the largest platform for podcast content, Zaagman writes that "a hard shift into end-to-end audio content aggregation and an advertising-based business model would require a fairly dramatic overhaul of their business model, organization, and brand."[28] Zaagman also explains that while Apple has attempted advertising-based models, the results have so far fallen flat.

Voice-based Recommendations

Siri, Echo, Alexa and other voice assistants are primed to become a dominant interface for recommendations as voice-based search continues to claim a more significant share of the total search market. Amazon's Alexa has already been integrated into the LG Smart InstaView refrigerator, which can be used to add items to your shopping list from Amazon Prime among numerous other tasks including recipe suggestions and playing music.

---

[28] Elliot Zaagman, "We need a Toutiao for podcasts," *Technode*, accessed March 7, 2018, https://technode.com/2018/03/06/bytedance-podcasts/.

Environment-based Recommendations

Perhaps the most visionary of emerging recommender systems is Google's patented environment-based recommender system. The tech behemoth has patented "advertising based on environmental conditions," which draws on environmental factors such as temperature and humidity collected through device sensors. In addition to climatic factors, the technology is said to gather light, sound and air composition and translate this information into criteria for what ads to serve users.

According to the official patent, "When determining what ads to serve to end users, the environmental factors can be used independently or in combination with the matching of keywords associated with the advertisements and keywords in user search queries."[29]

In other words, Google may intend to piece information about your online search activity together with your offline activities to push relevant advertisements. To bring this idea into focus, Google could, for example, pinpoint when you're at the beach based on climatic conditions. Armed with this information, Google could send beach-related recommendations based on your previous search behavior, including preferences for local restaurants and retail outlets. GPS location tracking technology,

---

[29] "Advertising based on environmental conditions," *United States Patent and Trademark Office*, accessed March 30, 2018, http://patft.uspto.gov/netacgi/nph-Parser?Sect1=PTO1&Sect2=HITOFF&d=PALL&p=1&u=%2Fnetahtml%2FPTO%2Fsrchnum.htm&r=1&f=G&l=50&s1=8,138,930.PN.&OS=PN/8,138,930&RS=PN/8,138,930/.

though, is adequately advanced to underwrite this type of knowledge-specific recommendation.

What about scenarios less reliant on location? When smoke drifts into the house from the BBQ cooking outside, will Amazon make ad recommendations based on your preference for grilled meat and vegetables? And will they make recommendations based on personal conversations, which TV channels you watch, and crying overheard by a linked device?

These questions are yet to be answered, and a filed patent is not a linear indication that Google will ship this technology in the future. A patent merely secures the intellectual protection of an internal company idea. The patent, though, does draw attention to the simple and early-stage sophistication of current recommender systems, which as we know, are largely based on binary likes and ordinal star ratings.

Recommendation-driven Story Arches

Personalization stands at the forefront of recommender systems' success so far, and a logical extrapolation of this trend is to go beyond recommending one item against another, to crafting content based on sophisticated personalization.

A commercial manifestation of this concept might be a TV series with multiple story arches that vary according to the reaction of the individual. Facial recognition, for example, could be used to collect a user's emotional ties to a particular protagonist. If

Gandalf in the Lord of the Rings is centimeters from death and the viewer is clearly disturbed by this scene, Gandalf may suddenly be spared through the viewer's 3-D glasses or viewing apparatus. Similarly, scenes may change to an alternative story arch based on the number of children in the audience through deep learning-backed face recognition technology that can detect the mean age of viewers.

FURTHER RESOURCES

Taking into account the promising developments of augmented reality, facial recognition, 5G networks, and dedicated deep learning processing chips, there are endless possibilities for recommender systems to evolve. Whether recommender systems excite or scare you, the best way to manage their influence and impact is to understand the architecture and algorithms that play on your personal data.

To learn more about developing your expertise in machine learning and data mining, you can find selected learning materials listed on the following pages.

These recommendations are personally curated and not generated by a sophisticated recommendation engine.

Recommender Systems: The Textbook

Author: Charu C. Aggarwal

Suggested Audience: All

This textbook is far and away the best resource that I've come across in the space of recommender systems and well worth the investment ($59 for the e-version and $55 for the hardcopy on Amazon) for anyone who wishes to proceed further in this field.

The Netflix Prize and Production Machine Learning Systems: An Insider Look

Format: Blog

Author: Mathworks

Suggested Audience: All

A very interesting blog article demonstrating how Netflix applies machine learning to form movie recommendations.

Recommender Systems

Format: Coursera course

Presenter: The University of Minnesota

Cost: Free 7-day trial or included with $49 USD Coursera subscription

Suggested Audience: All

Taught by the University of Minnesota, this Coursera specialization course covers fundamental recommender system techniques including content-based and collaborative filtering as well as non-personalized and project-association recommender systems.

Everybody Lies: Big Data, New Data, and What the Internet Can Tell Us About Who We Really Are

Format: E-book, book, audiobook

Author: Seth Stephens-Davidowitz

Drawing on his experience working for Google and knowledge of bizarre Google trends, author Seth Stephens-Davidowitz investigates common beliefs and tests them against big data and online search patterns to deliver digital truth serum as well as some surprising revelations about human behavior.

Amazon.com Recommendations Item-to-Item Collaborative Filtering

Format: Industry report

Author: Greg Linden, Brent Smith, and Jeremy York

Industry report on item-to-item collaborative filtering by Amazon.com.

Mining Massive Data Sets, Winter 2018

Format: Stanford University course video archive

Lecturer: Jure Leskovec

Video archive of the 2018 course Mining Massive Data Sets taught at Stanford by Jure Leskovec. Two weeks of this course are specifically dedicated to recommender systems. Available at https://stanford.io/2CfEd1g

Kaggle

Format: Online platform

Suggested Audience: All

Kaggle is an online community for data scientists and statisticians to access free datasets, join competitions, and simply hang out and talk about data. A great thing about Kaggle is that they offer free datasets for download. This saves you the time and effort in sourcing and tidying up your own dataset. Meanwhile, you also have access to discuss and problem-solve with other users on the forum about particular datasets. All datasets used in the exercises in this book can be downloaded for free from Kaggle.

Data and Goliath: The Hidden Battles to Collect Your Data and Control Your World

Format: E-book, book, audiobook

Author: Bruce Schneier

Suggested Audience: All

Regardless of your interest in private data security, this book is a must-read to understand the arguments against modern data surveillance. Of note to readers of this book, Schneier articulates the adverse effects of highly precise recommender systems which can do more damage than good in regards to customer loyalty for the companies that devise them.

The Power of Habit: Why We Do What We Do in Life and Business

Format: E-book, book, audiobook

Author: Charles Duhigg

Suggested Audience: All

While better classified under the self-help genre than machine learning, this book offers practical insight into human nature, which is a compatible and potentially valuable field for data scientists to study. I believe that readers will find Chapter 7 (How Target Knows What You Want Before You Do) of this book inspiring and insightful as it includes one of the most detailed accounts of the famous Target marketing campaign that could discern if a customer was pregnant—even before the customer's parents found out.

BUG BOUNTY

Thank you for reading this absolute beginners' introduction to recommender systems.

We offer a financial reward to readers for locating errors or bugs in this book. Some apparent errors could be mistakes made in interpreting a diagram or following along with the code in the book, so we invite all readers to contact the author first for clarification and a possible reward, before posting a one-star review! Just send an email to the author at **oliver.theobald@scatterplotpress.com** explaining the error or mistake you encountered.

This way, we can also supply further explanations and examples over email to calibrate your understanding, or in cases where you're right, and we're wrong, we offer a monetary reward through PayPal or Amazon gift card. This way you can make a tidy profit from your feedback, and we can update the book to improve the standard of content for future readers.

FROM THE AUTHOR

Thank you for purchasing this book. Recommender systems offer an exciting field of opportunity for budding data scientists, and you're now on the path to developing your own basic recommender systems.

I wish you all the best with your future career in data science. If you have any direct feedback about aspects of the book you strongly liked or dislike, please feel free to write to me at oliver.theobald@scatterplotpress.com. This feedback is highly valued, and I look forward to hearing from you.

If you enjoyed this book and would like to support the series, please feel free to leave a review. Reviews from readers weigh heavily on Amazon's recommender algorithm, so even one or two lines and a positive rating go a long way toward boosting our reach.

Oliver Theobald

October 2018

OTHER BOOKS BY THE AUTHOR

AI for Absolute Beginners
Published in 2023, this book is the complete guide for beginners to AI, including easy-to-follow breakdowns of natural language processing, generative AI, deep learning, recommender systems, and computer vision.

Generative AI Art for Beginners
Master the use of text prompts to generate stunning AI art in seconds.

ChatGPT Prompts Book
Maximize your results with ChatGPT using a series of proven text prompt strategies.

Machine Learning for Absolute Beginners
Learn the fundamentals of machine learning, explained in plain English.

Machine Learning with Python for Beginners
Progress your career in machine learning by learning how to code in Python and build your own prediction models to solve real-life problems.

Data Analytics for Absolute Beginners
Make better decisions using every variable with this deconstructed introduction to data analytics.

Statistics for Absolute Beginners
Master the fundamentals of inferential and descriptive statistics with a mix of practical demonstrations, visual examples, historical origins, and plain English explanations.

Python for Absolute Beginners
Master the essentials of Python from scratch with beginner-friendly guidance.

www.ingramcontent.com/pod-product-compliance
Lightning Source LLC
Chambersburg PA
CBHW031243050326
40690CB00007B/928